REVIVE US AGAIN

O.S. Hawkins

Revive Us, Again

BROADMAN PRESS
NASHVILLE, TENNESSEE

© Copyright 1990 • Broadman Press

All Rights Reserved

4250-96

ISBN: 0-8054-5096-3

Dewey Decimal Classification: 248.5

Subject Headings: WITNESSING // CHURCH

Library of Congress Catalog Number: 90-33218

Printed in the United States of America

Library of Congress Cataloging-in-Publication Data

Hawkins, O. S.
  Revive us again / O. S. Hawkins.
    p.   cm.
  ISBN 0-8054-5096-3
  1. Evangelistic work.   2. Witness bearing (Christianity)
  3. Fellowship—Religious aspects—Christianity.   I. Title.
  BV3790.H376   1990
  269'.2—dc20   90-33218
                                                             CIP

To
Gene A. Whiddon,
who is in heaven

My faithful deacon and devoted friend

"Your love has given me great joy and
encouragement, because you, brother,
have refreshed the hearts of the saints"
(Philem. 1:7).

Other Books by O. S. Hawkins

When Revival Comes (with Jack R. Taylor)
After Revival Comes
Clues to a Successful Life
Where Angels Fear to Tread
Tracing the Rainbow Through the Rain
Unmasked!
Jonah: Meeting the God of the Second Chance

Introduction

This book, *Revive Us Again,* capsulates in many respects my years in the pastorate. With all of my being I believe in a balanced ministry—evangelism, the equipping of the saints, social ministries, special ministries, and more. I am grateful to God that our church, the First Baptist Church of Fort Lauderdale, Florida, is recognized for its care and concern for every aspect of people's lives.

At Thanksgiving we serve perhaps the largest Thanksgiving dinner in the world, as many as seven thousand attend. We encourage everybody to come, not only at Thanksgiving, but all through the year. We are a church with an open door, without distinctions between race, color, or social standing. Our church baptizes more than five hundred persons a year.

There is nothing to compare with the power of the Holy Spirit when He is allowed to do His supernatural work in a church. This is the thrust of this book. There is an inseparable connection between the third person of the Trinity, the Holy Spirit, and revival. The church, whether a local church or the entire body of Christ, which comprises every true child of God, could not exist without the empowering of the Holy Spirit.

"This is my story, this is my song." In a sense this is almost two books. I originally wanted to call it *Like a Mighty Army,* but I remembered that my neighbor, Dr. James Kennedy of the Coral Ridge Presbyterian Church, has a book by that title. So my publisher and I decided on *Revive Us Again*. That title should strike into our hearts.

Let me quote the late Dr. C. E. Matthews, who at one time headed up my denomination's evangelism ministry:

> The author (Matthews), while filling a speaking engagement in a northern city, heard a report on evangelism. The report included 116 Baptist churches with an average of four baptisms per church for the preaching year. The next day he (Matthews) was present in an evangelistic service where some two thousand young people were present. The speaker on the occasion brought a good message. He stated that the movement which he represented had "witnessed the sweeping of thousands into the kingdom of God." The next day one of the officials of the movement (which was ecumenical in its aspect) said to the author (Matthews): "I appreciated seeing you in our services yesterday. What do you think of our movement?"
>
> I answered, "It is doomed to failure."
>
> "Why do you say that?" he asked.
>
> I replied: "Because it bypasses the churches."
>
> He said, "The churches up here are dead."
>
> "You had better resurrect them," I replied, "if your work is to be permanent. That is what He is crying out to His churches throughout the world today: Repent and be revived! Every church needs a revival. A revival is as essential to the Christian's heart as rain is to the ground. A genuine heaven-sent revival of the Christian religion is the supreme need of this hour. A hunger for God should be in the heart of every child of God as Christians face their adversary who seems to be parading up and down this earth

as a bloodthirsty, roaring lion, seeking whom he may devour. God is ready to send that needed revival when the churches are ready to receive it."[1]

The necessity for revival has not changed from the first century until now. The Psalmist prayed, "Will you not *revive us again*, that your people may rejoice in you?" (Ps. 85:6, author's italics). Should this not be the heart cry of the church of the Lord Jesus as we approach the twenty-first century? Should we not beseech heaven with this plea? "Revive us again!" When so many pastors' pulpits and professors' lecterns have become dispensaries of human philosophies; when many of our educational systems have become citadels of shameless atheism, agnosticism, and blatant humanism; and when some high-profile ministries have sunk to the depths of undisciplined corruption is it not time to pray, "Revive us again, that your people may rejoice in you"?

When from the media we hear the thoughtless cries of a thousand voices calling our children to life-styles of godlessness and when so many churches settle to tolerate comfortably a declining civilization while all the time adjusting their demands to accommodate indifference, I am positive it is time for real revival. Nothing else will do.

With the above in mind, this volume is offered. The hope of our world is in the person of our Lord and Savior Jesus Christ and invested in the local New Testament church. Don't sell the church short, because the gates of hell will not prevail against her. As the church draws near to the conclusion of two thousand years of ministry and outreach, her urgent necessity is revival, to live again. Thus, through these pages we return to the church's birth in Jerusalem on the Day of Pentecost and seek to incorporate twenty-first century methods to this first-century message which never changes.

The first "revival meeting" I preached as a young preacher in Texas was at a small church on the outskirts of Fort Worth. It was a sizzling, hot summer, and the services were outdoors by an old water well. Every night we sang our revival theme song. I had never heard the song before that week, but in all these years there is hardly a day I have not thought of it. It is still my constant daily prayer, and only heaven has recorded how many times I have sung it in my heart during my personal devotions. My prayer is as you read the following pages you will make this your passionate plea to the Father:

> We praise Thee, O God! for the Son of Thy love,
> For Jesus who died, and is now gone above.
>
> We praise Thee, O God! for Thy Spirit of light,
> Who hath shown us our Saviour, and scatter'd our night.
>
> All glory and praise to the Lamb that was slain,
> Who has borne all our sins, and hath cleans'd ev'ry
>   stain.
>
> Revive us again; fill each heart with Thy love;
> May each soul be rekindled with fire from above.
>
> Hallelujah! Thine the glory, Hallelujah! amen;
> Hallelujah! Thine the glory, Revive us again.
>
> Lyrics by WILLIAM P. MACKAY

Signs of Revival:
What Makes a Great Church

What makes a church great? This question is dependent upon whether we are referring to a great church in the eyes of people or a great church in the eyes of God. Often in the eyes of people a great church is determined by a stupendous financial program. However, there are many churches with huge endowments which are dead and listless.

Others might claim that vast physical facilities make a great church. While this may be true from people's views, there are churches with mammoth, magnificent edifices with only a handful of people. You can find in the downtown areas of most major cities, churches that were once vibrant and alive that are now dead and dying, but with awe-inspiring physical facilities. Still others would insist that a great church is made up of those with elite social standing. While this may be true, according to people, it is not so in the eyes of God.

The secret to a great church in the eyes of God is found in the second chapter of Acts with the birth of the church. It includes four vital elements. The first element is *participation*. These early believers were "all together" (Acts 2:1).

They found their strength in participation with God. There has never been a great church that has not captured this element of participation. Second, there is the element of *proclamation*. These early believers preached the Word of God. Peter stood up on the day of Pentecost, took a text from the scroll of Joel, and preached the gospel of Jesus Christ, boldly and unashamedly. Third, there is the element of *preservation*. The Bible tells us they "continued steadfastly" in the apostles' teachings. They "devoted themselves" to prayer and fellowship. People did not come through "one door of the early church and out the back." They had captured the element of preservation. Finally, there is the element of *propagation*. They went everywhere witnessing, and the Bible states, "the Lord added to their number daily those who were being saved" (Acts 2:47). Any church that aspires to be great in the eyes of God must be characterized by these four vital elements.

Today, the church of the Lord Jesus Christ must raise up her head and remember who she is. I hope we do not want to be viewed in our cities as some kind of religious, country club or some sort of second-class organization that gets thrown a bone from the city's civic community from time to time. No! The church is not some insignificant, musty-smelling mausoleum trying to hold onto a few traditional values of the past. The most important organization to the future of any area ought to be the local New Testament church. It ought not to be the Tourist Bureau, the Chamber of Commerce, the Downtown Development Authority, or any other such organizations. It ought to be the local New Testament church planted in the heart of the community, making a difference for Jesus' sake.

The church was born in the city of Jerusalem in the first-century A.D. People from all over the known world gathered there for the Feast of Pentecost. As many as one million Jews descended upon the city for the annual celebration. But on that particular day, 120 believers became the center of attention. The Feast of Pentecost had been observed for 1,500 years. Always held fifty days after the Passover, it was designed to celebrate the arrival of the Israelites to Mount Sinai after their deliverance from Egypt. During that feast God had the attention of the city and ultimately the world, and through one local body of believers, turned the world upside down. How the church ought to pray in these days, "Lord, do it again!"

I repeat, "What makes a church great in the eyes of God?" Participation, proclamation, preservation, and propagation make it great. Every church ought to exhibit all four. There are some churches which have participation but no proclamation. Others are strong on proclamation but have no participation. Others have participation and proclamation but no preservation. And yet others have the first three but no program of propagation of the gospel. Great churches are known by balanced ministries and have all four elements found in Acts 2. They live together in love and unity, are filled with the Holy Spirit, make much of the Word of God, have ministries to preserve new converts, and continue to exist for those beyond their four walls.

Contents

1. Participation . . . 17

2. Proclamation . . . 46

3. Preservation. . . . 91

4. Propagation 113

   Notes 126

1
Participation

John was a successful oral surgeon. He had all the outward appearances of the epitome of the South Florida baby boomer with the world by its tail. That is, until his world came crashing in on him, and for the first time a situation arose which could not be handled by his own ingenuity or clever maneuvering. Divorce began looming on the horizon and eventually became reality. In the ensuing months, the dark clouds of despair and loneliness began to hover, and recurring thoughts of suicide arose all too often.

Reading the paper one afternoon, John noticed an advertisement: A Divorce Recovery Workshop at the First Baptist Church. *Divorce recovery?* he thought. *That's what I need, but it would mean becoming vulnerable! And . . . First Baptist Church? Aren't those the kind of people who are so narrow-minded that a gnat could stand on the bridge of their nose and peck out both of their eyes?*

But real desperation has a way of breaking down pride and preconceived ideas. Encouraged by Rick, a Christian friend, John attended the workshop. From the very first he quickly discovered that something and Someone could truly bring hope and healing.

Week after week as Anne led the workshop, John's wounds began to heal. At God's appointed time, Bill began to help. He took his evangelism training team to see John, and John received the gift of eternal life. At this writing, John is on an evangelism training team himself, involved in leading others to a saving faith in Jesus Christ. We are learning there are thousands of "Johns" in our city waiting, just waiting, for someone to be Christ's hand extended to them.

What if David had not placed that ad? What if Rick had not given a word of encouragement? What if Anne had remained bitter after her divorce fifteen years earlier and had not allowed the experience to result in a ministry that has reached thousands? What if Bill had not dropped by and shared the good news of eternal life?

What if our local expression of the body of Christ, the church, was not functioning together in love and unity? Until the church of our Lord comes together in genuine love and unity, exercising its ministry gifts for the edification of the entire body, we have no right to pray, "Revive us again!"

[1]When the day of Pentecost came, they were all together in one place. [2]Suddenly a sound like the blowing of a violent wind came from heaven and filled the whole house where they were sitting. [3]They saw what seemed to be tongues of fire that separated and came to rest on each of them. [4]All of them were filled with the Holy Spirit and began to speak in other tongues as the Spirit enabled them.

[5]Now there were staying in Jerusalem God-fearing Jews from every nation under heaven. [6]When they heard this sound, a crowd came together in bewilderment, because

each one heard them speaking in his own language. [7]Utterly amazed, they asked: "Are not all these men who are speaking Galileans? [8]Then how is it that each of us hears them in his own native language? [9]Parthians, Medes and Elamites; residents of Mesopotamia, Judea and Cappadocia, Pontus and Asia, [10]Phrygia and Pamphylia, Egypt and the parts of Libya near Cyrene; visitors from Rome [11](both Jews and converts to Judaism); Cretans and Arabs—we hear them declaring the wonders of God in our own tongues!" [12]Amazed and perplexed, they asked one another, "What does this mean?"

[13]Some, however, made fun of them and said, "They have had too much wine" (Acts 2:1-13).

Note the word *all*. They were *all* together, *all* in one accord, *all* in one place, and *all* filled. This participation involved two tremendously important ingredients—unity and unction.

Unity

The members of the early church found its strength in participation with one another. They were "all together" (Acts 2:1). They were united and not divided. They decided to stay together as well as pray together. Unity is one of the single most important factors in church growth. We are talking about unity and not uniformity. Cults emphasize uniformity, while the church emphasizes unity. The church is the picture of a quartet with each member singing different parts of the same song but blending together in perfect harmony.

What was the real phenomenon occurring on the day the church was born? It was a miracle of sound and sight. There

Not the signs but the results are needed again.

"Lord, do it again."

was a miracle of *sound:* "Suddenly a sound like the blowing of a violent wind came from heaven and filled the whole house where they were sitting" (Acts 2:2). The *sound* of the wind was the sign of the Holy Spirit. Earlier Jesus taught in his conversation with Nicodemus, "The wind blows wherever it pleases. You hear its sound, but you cannot tell where it comes from or where it is going. So it is with everyone born of the Spirit" (John 3:8). There was also the miracle of *sight.* "They saw what seemed to be tongues of fire that separated and came to rest on each of them" (Acts 2:3). There were cloven tongues of fire which, like the wind, was the sign of the Holy Spirit. Fire that consumes. Oh how our Lord desires to consume us as His church.

There is plenty of talk in church circles today about seeing Pentecost repeated. How many times have we heard phrases such as, "They had a Pentecost at such and such church." If Pentecost is repeated there will be some signs. We will hear the sound of a rushing, mighty wind and see cloven tongues of fire appearing above each head. People will speak in *glossa* (languages) and *dialektos* (dialects). Why are we not seeing this phenomenon in the church today? There is no need for Pentecost to be repeated. It was a one-time event.

The coming of the Holy Spirit to indwell the believers and never to leave them, just like Bethlehem, was a one-time event and never needs to be repeated. It was like Calvary which was a one-time event and never needs to be repeated. Pentecost is the same. At Bethlehem, we see God *with* us. At Calvary, we see God *for* us. At Pentecost, we see God *in* us. For a Christian to pray, "Lord, send the Holy Spirit just like you did on the Day of Pentecost," would be the same as praying, "Lord, send Jesus to Bethlehem to be born of a virgin." He already has. It would be the same as praying, "Lord, send Jesus out to Calvary to die on a cross for our sins." He already has! Pentecost was a one-time event when the Holy Spirit came to indwell the believers, never to leave them and to empower them for service.

Note that the blessing on the Day of Pentecost came "suddenly" (Acts 2:2). It was not obtained through a process of growth or development. No one taught anyone else how to do what happened. It did not evolve out of one's own mental attitudes. It was the sovereign, supernatural gift of the Father upon each person. No one was excluded (see Acts 2:3). It was not manifested by merit. It was the work of God. It came "suddenly," and the effect was that "all of them were filled with the Holy Spirit" (Acts 2:4).

One of the problems of the twentieth century is that it has lost its expectancy. It is amazing how many events came about in the early church "suddenly." They seemed to live in anticipation of the unexpected. In Acts 2 the early believers were not waiting until they became worthy. They were praying and waiting, and "suddenly" the Spirit came.

Think of the shepherds living in the fields, keeping watch over their flocks at night:

An angel of the Lord appeared to them, and the glory of the Lord shone around them, and they were terrified. But the angel said to them, "Do not be afraid. I bring you good news of great joy that will be for all the people. Today in the town of David a Savior has been born to you; he is Christ the Lord. This will be a sign to you: You will find a baby wrapped in strips of cloth and lying in a manger."

Suddenly a great company of the heavenly host appeared with the angel, praising God and saying, "Glory to

God in the highest, and on earth peace to men on whom his favor rests" (Luke 2:9-14, author's italics).

Think of the apostle Paul on the Damascus road. The Bible records:

Meanwhile, Saul was still breathing out murderous threats against the Lord's disciples. He went to the high priest and asked him for letters to the synagogues in Damascus, so that if he found any there who belonged to the Way, whether men or women, he might take them as prisoners to Jerusalem. As he neared Damascus on his journey, *suddenly* a light from heaven flashed around him (Acts 9:1-3, author's italics).

Think of Silas and Paul in prison at Philippi. The Bible records:

About midnight Paul and Silas were praying and singing hymns to God, and the other prisoners were listening to them. *Suddenly* there was such a violent earthquake that the foundations of the prison were shaken. At once all the prison doors flew open, and everybody's chains came loose (Acts 16:25-26, author's italics).

Oh, the possibility of those of us who live in the realm of expecting the unexpected!

On the day the church was born, the believers were "all together in one place" (Acts 2:1). They sensed a ministry of attendance. They had felt that ministry since earlier in the upper room when Thomas was "not there when Jesus came." Now, they were in their place, "all together in one place." The church today would sense more power if its members lived in anticipation and were all together in one place.

Every layperson in every church has a ministry of attendance. One of the saddest verses in all the Bible is recorded in John 20:24 where the Scripture reveals, "Thomas . . . was not with the disciples when Jesus came." How urgent it is to be in one's place at the time of worship. I have often wondered where Thomas was that day. Wherever he was was not really the central concern; the point was, he was *not where he should have been when Jesus came*. Like Thomas, we are missing out when we are not fulfilling our ministry of attendance. The Lord brought not only His *presence* into the group that day, but also His *peace*. One never knows when he is not in his place if Jesus will pass by in tremendous power and presence. I am convinced that the actual reason Thomas was not there when Jesus came was the identical reason so many people in so many churches today do not fulfill their ministry of attendance. They simply do not expect Jesus to be there! A large percentage of church members attend as if they were going to some sort of committee meeting or town council meeting, without any thought that Jesus is actually passing by. Each of us has an awesome responsibility and a "ministry of attendance" at our own local church.

There are so many people in church today who want to "hear" a mighty, rushing wind or "see" cloven tongues of fire. This was an event never to be repeated. I am not claiming that God could not do this again, but I am saying it certainly seems that He has not chosen to manifest Himself in such a way today. God may move dramatically to work in our lives which involve the senses—what we can see, hear, touch, smell, or taste; or, more likely, He will use gentle breezes and whispers.

Remember Elijah? The Lord commanded him,

"Go out and stand on the mountain in the presence of the Lord, for the Lord is about to pass by."

Then a great and powerful wind tore the mountains apart and shattered the rocks before the Lord, but the Lord was not in the wind. After the wind there was an earthquake, but the Lord was not in the earthquake. After the earthquake came a fire, but the Lord was not in the fire. And after the fire came a gentle whisper (1 Kings 19:11-12).

Elijah was in desperate need to hear from God. There was a mighty wind, but God was not in the wind. There was an earthquake, but God was not in the earthquake. There was a fire, but God was not in the fire. And finally the Bible says, "a gentle whisper, a still small voice."[1] This is generally the way it happens to me, "a still small voice in my heart."

One of the real characteristics of the first-century church was unity. They were in one accord, in one place. In fact, it is amazing how, as we read through the Book of Acts, they continued to find their strength in participation with each other. They began in Acts 1:14: "They all joined together constantly in prayer, along with the women and Mary the mother of Jesus, and his brothers." They continued in Acts 2:1: "When the day of Pentecost came, they were all together in one place." After the day of Pentecost the Bible records, "Every day they continued to meet together in the temple courts. They broke bread in their homes and ate together with glad and sincere hearts" (Acts 2:46).

After Peter and John had been arrested, the Bible emphasizes, "When they heard this, they raised their voices together in prayer to God. 'Sovereign Lord,' they said, 'you made the heaven and the earth and the sea, and everything in them'" (Acts 4:24). When deep fear came upon them after the death of Ananias and Sapphira the Bible records, "The apostles performed many miraculous signs and wonders among the people. And all the believers used to meet together in Solomon's Colonnade" (Acts 5:12). The secret to the growth of the early church was its living together in love and unity.

The most important fact is not what they saw or heard but that they were "all together." They were in one accord, and God met them in that place. Participation, unity, and unction were manifest. They were as different as people in churches today, but God cemented them together and did great and mighty works through them. Look at those in that group. Peter was there. He was so boisterous and the one who denied our Lord before a maiden. Thomas the doubter was present. John and James were in the midst, having been so selfish in wanting to have the number one and number two positions in the Kingdom. There were forgiven adulterers and also tax collectors. You name it, and they were there—Joseph of Arimathea and civic leaders like Nicodemus. They were all different but their secret was they were "all together" in one place. There was participation in unity. They found strength in participation with each other.

Unity was the key to the outpouring of God's Spirit. This group was so diverse. In fact, probably much more diverse than most churches are today. They had the richest of the rich in Joseph of Arimathea and the poorest of the poor in the widow. Yet, they were "all together." There seemed to be no petty bickering, no silly jealousy. So many churches today are filled with people who are backbiting and murmuring. Many of us ought to stop worrying about getting a blessing and start worrying about being a blessing. The secret of this Jerusalem church was participation. They found their strength in participation with one another. This is the real key to a great church in the eyes of God. Unity was the theme. They were "all together in one place."

They not only found their strength in participation with one another, but in participation with God. "*All* of them were filled with the Holy Spirit" (Acts 2:4, author's italics). Not some of them but all of them! They had been baptized, indwelt, and sealed by the Holy Spirit; now they were filled by Him. The emphasis in Acts 2 is on the filling of the Holy Spirit. This puts us under the spotlight of the principle of "becoming before doing," for what we do is always determined by who we are and what we are. While baptism with the Holy Spirit was a once-and-for-all encounter, the filling of the Holy Spirit is to be repeated over and over again. This is what makes a church great in the eyes of God—a Spirit-filled membership where Jesus is the Lord of every life. At conversion we have the Holy Spirit. When we are filled, the Holy Spirit has us!

The work of the Holy Spirit in our lives involves several factors. It involves the *baptism with the Holy Spirit*. First Corinthians 12:13 says: "For we were all baptized by one Spirit into one body—whether Jews or Greeks, slave or free—and we are all given the one Spirit to drink."

There is also the *indwelling of the Holy Spirit*. Romans 8:9 says: "You, however, are controlled not by the sinful nature but by the Spirit, if the Spirit of God lives in you. And if anyone does not have the Spirit of Christ, he does not belong to Christ."

Then there is the *sealing of the Holy Spirit*. Ephesians 1:13-14 states:

And you also were included in Christ when you heard the word of truth, the gospel of your salvation. Having believed, you were marked in him with a seal, the promised Holy Spirit, who is a deposit guaranteeing our inheritance until the redemption of those who are God's possession—to the praise of his glory.

Next comes the *filling of the Holy Spirit* found in Ephesians 5:18: "Do not get drunk on wine, which leads to debauchery. Instead, be filled with the Spirit." The filling is conditional upon our surrender to Jesus as Lord.

There is also the *anointing of the Holy Spirit*. At the Lord's baptism, the Holy Spirit anointed Him. The anointing is a special touch for a special task. Thank God for the anointing! No preacher ought to preach without asking God for "fresh oil"—the anointing. No singer ought to sing without asking God for the anointing. No teacher ought to teach the Bible without asking God for the anointing.

What is the command of the Bible in regards to the Holy Spirit? Is it to be *baptized* with the Holy Spirit? No! There is not one command in Scripture to be baptized with the Holy Spirit. In fact, if we are saved, the Bible teaches us we have already been baptized with the Holy Spirit. Are we commanded to be *indwelt* by the Holy Spirit? No! Is the command, then, to be *sealed* with the Holy Spirit? Again, the answer is no. The command of Scripture in regards to the Holy Spirit is to "be filled with the Spirit" (Eph. 5:18).

The filling of the Holy Spirit is a command. The word translated into the English *be filled* is the word *plerousthe* in the original language. Every verb has a number, tense, voice, and mood. When we look at this word *be filled* in Ephesians 5:18, we find that the number is plural. The tense is present, continuous action. The voice is passive, meaning that the subject doesn't act. It is acted upon. The mood is imperative. There is no option. Therefore, properly translated, the command to be filled in Ephesians 5:18 is saying, "all of you must always be filled with the Holy Spirit."

What makes a church great in the eyes of God? The first element is participation. This involves *unity* (participation with each other) and *unction* (participation with God).

Unction

What actually happened in Acts 2? It was a phenomenon! They spoke in other languages. Is this happening today? What transpired? It is important to grasp what the Bible really reveals about this incredible event. After all, if our experience does not match the Word of God, it is not valid. As we come before God's Word, we should try to strip away any preconceived prejudices and simply want to know, "What does the Bible say about this happening?"

Some argue, "I don't care what the Bible says. I know what I have experienced." They are subjective, believing more in their feelings than the inspired, written Word of God. In this study we are not preoccupied with the "charismatic" view. He usually claims if you are really filled with the Holy Spirit, the evidence is you will speak in tongues, since he feels that is a sign of the filling. Nor are we interested in what the charisphobiac declares. He usually argues it is all of the devil, which puts him in a terrible position. We want to know, "What does God's Word say?" How can we "rightly divide the word of truth" and understand what is actually said about this phenomenal event?

Like those men and women who were there that day, we ask, "What does this mean?" (Acts 2:12). With an open Bible, the answer is extremely plain. We never have to be afraid of what the Bible declares, regardless of whether or not it fits our preconceived ideas. The bottom line is the Word of God, not my experience or my pet ideas.

Many people cry, "I've had a Pentecostal experience." Well, if so, that experience will line up and measure up with Scripture. We should look at every experience we have through the Word of God and test its validity. After all, John exhorts us to "test the spirits to see whether they are from God, because many false prophets have gone out into the world" (1 John 4:1). We do not have to be afraid of what the Word of God says because the Word is profitable.

In first-century Palestine the spoken language was Aramaic, and the written language was Greek. Alexander the Great had conquered the known world, and the Greek language had spread as a universal language. Therefore, when the New Testament was written, it was written in the Greek language. Our task is to find the most ancient Greek manuscripts we can and go back as close to the original autographs as possible. We should want to study the language in which Luke wrote as he penned the word in the book of Acts. The Greek word in Acts 2:4, which is translated *tongues,* is the word *glossa.* It means language. It means *known* language. In fact, we receive our English word *glossary* from this Greek word. These were languages foreign to the speaker which he had never heard, but by which he was supernaturally empowered to speak as a result of the Holy Spirit. The phenomenon happened with the Jews at Pentecost in Acts 2. It happened again with the disciples of John the Baptist at Ephesus in Acts 19. Each time the word *glossa* is used, Jews were present, and unbelieving Jews were in the background.

What happened at Pentecost was that these were all languages unknown to the speakers and spoken at that particular time in demonstration of the entrance of the age of grace.

They were not unknown languages. In fact, we do not read in the New Testament about an "unknown tongue." You might ask, "What about 1 Corinthians 14:2?" This Scripture says, "For anyone who speaks in a tongue does not speak to men but to God. Indeed, no one understands him; he utters mysteries with his spirit." If you will read carefully, the word *unknown* is in italics, indicating that it is not found in the Greek manuscripts but inserted by translators. *The New International Version* omits the word *unknown,* and rightly so. These languages spoken on the Day of Pentecost were *known* dialects. Everyone heard them speaking in their own language (Acts 2:8).

It is interesting that this same word *glossa* used in Acts 2:4 is also found in Revelation 5:9. In this picture of heaven, we read these words:

And they sang a new song:

"You are worthy to take the scroll
    and to open its seals,
  because you were slain,
    and with your blood you purchased
      men for God
    from every tribe and *language* and
      people and nation" (author's italics).

It is also found in Revelation 7:9:

> After this I looked and there before me was a great multi-
> tude that no one could count, from every nation, tribe, peo-
> ple and *language,* standing before the throne and in front
> of the Lamb. They were wearing white robes and were hold-
> ing palm branches in their hands (author's italics).

The word means language. It is linguistic and not some in-
coherent babbling.

What is the difference between the words which are
translated in the English word *tongue* in Acts 2:4 and the
words translated *language* in Acts 2:6,8? In verse 4 the
word is *glossa,* and in verses 6 and 8 the word is *dialektos.*
Verse 8 is translated by the English word *tongue* in the
King James Version, but properly translated in *The New
International Version* as *language.* This latter word means
dialect.[2] What we have is the word for *language* in Acts 2:4
and the word for *dialect* in Acts 2:6,8.

So what do I mean? What happened? People gathered
from all over the known world for the Feast of Pentecost.
There were between twelve and seventeen (depending on
the translation) different languages represented at that
feast on that particular day. The miracle was in the hearing. They heard not just in their own language, but in the
dialect which they spoke! For example, in our own church,
we have a man from Alabama who is a good friend of a man
from Brooklyn, who are both friends of a man from London,
England. They all speak English, but each of their dialects
is as different as daylight and dark!

What happened on the Day of Pentecost were known
languages spoken in dialects. There is no possibility that
Acts 2 refers to any type of unknown gibberish. This was
not merely a bunch of different syllables all thrown to-

gether like so many people try to teach others today. It passed the test of linguistics. These were known languages of the day, and the miracle was not in the speaking as much as it was in the hearing. No one was teaching anyone else how to speak it. They were hearing it not only in their own language, but the miracle was they heard it in their own dialect!

It is intriguing to pay attention to those who were assembled there that day. "Now there were staying in Jerusalem God-fearing Jews from every nation under heaven" (Acts 2:5). This tongue was a sign/gift to the Jewish nation. This is what Paul means in 1 Corinthians 14:21-22:

> In the law it is written:
>
>> "Through men of strange tongues
>>> and through the lips of foreigners
>> I will speak to this people,
>>> but even then they will not listen to me,"
>
> says the Lord.
>
> Tongues, then, are a sign, not for believers but for unbelievers; prophecy, however, is for believers, not for unbelievers.

This people refers to the Jews. It was a sign to the unbelievers, who were present whenever tongues occurred in the New Testament. It consisted of known languages and was addressed to God in praise. They did not preach the gospel in tongues in Acts 2; they spoke about the wonderful works of God (Acts 2:11). After grabbing the attention of the crowd, Peter stood up and preached a gospel sermon in the known language of the day. An interpreter was not needed in this phenomenon in Acts 2.

The result was amazing. "Utterly amazed, they asked: 'Are not all these men who are speaking Galileans?'" (Acts 2:7). People began to ask, "How can these men speak these different *glossa* and *dialektos* (languages and dialects)? They are neither educated nor traveled. They are not from the universities or the seminaries. Look at them! They are rough, crude, callous-handed Galilean fishermen. How is it that when they speak we hear in our language of the wonderful works of God?" We must remember that this event occurred long before the days of the art of linguistics. It was difficult to learn foreign languages in the first-century world. One had to live in a particular country for a considerable period of time. And yet, these Galileans, untrained and unlearned, were speaking in foreign languages and dialects about the wonderful works of God.

The miracle was not just in the speaking, but it was in the hearing. Where is the miracle at Pentecost being repeated today? Some preach we need another Pentecost, so they go to an altar, speak a bunch of unintelligible syllables, perhaps jump up and down, and claim they have had the "Pentecostal experience." It is plain what will happen if you have a Pentecostal experience; you will hear the sound of a rushing wind, see cloven tongues of fire, and speak in known languages and dialects which you have never heard, and people will hear in their native language without needing an interpreter! Where is this happening today?

What happened here? Why doesn't it seem to be happening anymore? Some insist it is happening. But the truth is that it is not happening as it did on the Day of Pentecost, manifested with wind, fire, and languages. What was transpiring here? This was the beginning of a new dispensation of the Holy Spirit, the age of grace. What did God do at the beginning of each new dispensation? He introduced it with wonders, signs, and miracles which were not necessarily ever repeated.

This is true all through the Word of God. For example, when God created the earth, all matter, He did it with wonders and signs and miracles. He spoke, and it came into being. But since the early chapters of Genesis, not one single atom of matter has been created out of nothing. The same is true when God began the dispensation of the Law. It was ushered in with wonders and signs and miracles which have not been repeated. There was the parting of the Red Sea and the parting of the Jordan. There was a cloud by day and a pillar of fire by night, which led the children of Israel. There was also the manna falling from heaven. This is not to deny that God could do any of these miracles again, but He obviously does not work in exactly that manner today. There is only one dispensation remaining. It will come at the end of this age of grace with the second coming of our Lord Jesus Christ and will be accompanied by signs, wonders, and miracles that the world has yet to see.[3]

God can do whatever He wants—except violate His own will and character. He can create something out of nothing anytime He desires. He can part an ocean and rain down manna from heaven. But He is not doing such today as He did at the beginning of these dispensations. This certainly does not imply that He is any less of a God. He is always the same—yesterday, today, and forever.

Pentecost marked the beginning of the church age, the age of the Holy Spirit, the age of grace. And like other dispensations, it was accompanied with signs, wonders, and miracles (rushing, mighty winds and flaming tongues of fire, as well as *glossa* and *dialektos* spoken by unlearned men).

As the Book of Acts continues, we will see this third sign of speaking in languages, when the gospel is preached for the Gentiles at the home of Cornelius, a Roman centurion at Caesarea (Acts 10). Describing this event, Peter says, "So if God gave them *the same gift* as he gave us, who believed in the Lord Jesus Christ, who was I to think that I could oppose God!" (Acts 11:17, author's italics). It's emphasized that it was the "same gift." What happened in Acts 10 at Caesarea was the same thing that happened at Pentecost. That is, it was *glossa* and *dialektos!*

We see the identical thing again in Acts 19 when the gospel is preached at Ephesus, the great capital city of the Roman province of Asia. They magnified the Lord with *glossa*—known languages. It was not unintelligible babbling. This is not what *we think* happened at Pentecost, Caesarea, and Ephesus; it is what the Bible clearly teaches when we study what it actually says. All of us should be concerned more about what God's Word says than what someone else says about God's Word or some experience that may not measure alongside God's Word.

In 1 Corinthians 13:8, Paul says *glossa* shall cease. That is in and of itself. Some believe that like signs, which accompanied the Mosaic dispensation and the age of grace, have not been seen again in plentitude. When Paul said in 1 Corinthians 13 that knowledge and prophecy would cease, he used the word *katargeō,* which means to make idle, inoperative. It is the same word employed in 1 Corinthians 13:11, where the Bible states we "put childish ways behind." However, when Paul, in the same context states that *glossa* will cease, he uses the word *pausontai* which means automatically ceased of themselves. The Bible prophesied that there was coming a time when these gifts would cease. Prophecy and knowledge would simply cease, but tongues would cease *in and of themselves*. We cannot argue this. What we can argue is when this time was or will be. Many believe that such gifts as *glossa* and *dialektos* ceased with the completion of the New Testament.

We now have the complete revelation of God (the Bible), which makes fragmentary revelation pointless. Perhaps this is what Paul refers to in 1 Corinthians 13:10, when he writes, "but when perfection comes, the imperfect disappears." What is perfect? It is the inerrant, infallible Word of the living God. Then what does he mean when he declares that "the imperfect disappears" in the last part of verse 10? These gifts belonged to the infancy of the church, and as the church matured they were no longer needed. This is the reason for the next verse, which goes, "When I was a child, . . . I thought like a child, I reasoned like a child. When I became a man, I put childish ways behind me" (1 Cor. 13:11).

Did this particular sign/gift cease? It should be noted that one of Paul's earliest epistles was the first epistle written to the Corinthian church in or around 55 A.D. It was here, 1 Corinthians 12–14, that he spoke regarding *glossa* and stated in 1 Corinthians 13:8 that glossa would cease. After writing this epistle, Paul wrote the Roman letter, the marvelous doctrinal treatise of the Christian faith, and tongues were never mentioned. After Paul wrote that epistle, he penned 2 Corinthians, and again tongues were never mentioned. After Paul wrote 1 Corinthians, the sign of tongues is not mentioned again. Then he wrote Ephesians, the cyclical letter to the church of Asia, and once again there is not one reference to *glossa*. After Paul wrote 1 Corinthians, he wrote Colossians, 1 Thessalonians, 2 Thessalonians, 1 Timothy, 2 Timothy, Titus, and Philemon. In all these books not one word is mentioned about these *glossa* or *dialektos*. Why? Many believe it is as Paul wrote in 1 Corinthians 13:8 that *glossa* has ceased.[4]

What is my point? If tongues are as important as certain people attempt to make them to be today, they would have found their place in the letters to the various first-century churches. The only church to which the subject was addressed during the early days of the church age was to a church that was carnal and immature (see 1 Cor. 3). Others claim it is their prayer language. If it were as important as many people try to make it, when the disciples asked the Lord, "Lord, teach us to pray" (Luke 11:1), Jesus would surely have mentioned it.

Ironically, men throughout this age of grace who have been the most mightily used of God never spoke in *glossa* and *dialektos*. They follow the likes of Augustine, Savonarola, Wycliffe, Luther, Calvin, Wesley, Finney, Moody, Spurgeon, Sunday, Graham, and the list continues.

What is the phenomenon of Pentecost that needs to be repeated? Is it the wind? Is it the flaming fire? Is it the *glossa* and *dialektos?* No! It is the filling! All through Acts we read repeatedly that they were filled with the Holy Spirit. That is what we need—the filling of God's Holy Spirit. *At conversion we have the Holy Spirit. At the filling He has us!* And what happened? As they spoke in these other languages and dialects, the people heard them speaking in their own language and dialect. They spoke of the amazing wonders of God and certainly got the attention of the crowd. These tongues did not save a soul; they were attention getters. Three thousand people were saved, and the church was born when the preacher, Simon Peter, stood and preached the Lord Jesus Christ.

Revival comes through *participation* with God in the filling of His Holy Spirit. But what exactly is the real proof of being filled with God's Holy Spirit? The proof is evidenced in Ephesians 5:19-21. We will recall that the command of God is found in Ephesians 5:18, "be filled with the Spirit." The following verse will present the *inward* evidence. That is, how will *you* know? There will be a song in your heart!

The next verse gives us the *upward* evidence. That is, how will *God* know? Of course God knows everything, but the evidence is in thankfulness. We will have a heart full of thanksgiving and praise. The *outward* evidence is in the following verse. How will *others* know? By our spirit of submission one to another.

Inward Evidence

What is the inward evidence that one is being filled with the Holy Spirit? If God's command is in Ephesians 5:18, the inward evidence is in Ephesians 5:19, "Speak to one another with psalms, hymns and spiritual songs. Sing and make music in your heart to the Lord." What is the evidence? It is singing, even if you can't carry a tune in a bucket. This is the inward evidence of the fullness of God's Holy Spirit. We cannot stay filled with the Holy Spirit without singing. In the original text there is no period after verse 18. This is where we find the difference in Christianity and other world religions. If you look at the followers of Buddha they may have their impressive temples, but they have no song in their hearts. The Hindus may have their mantras, but they have no song in their hearts. Islam may pride itself in its morality, but they have no song in their hearts. When we are filled with the Holy Spirit, one of the sure proofs is joy. We are joyful inside. I love the title of that old song, "With a Song in My Heart." Even though we may be like Paul and Silas in a Philippian jail at midnight, we cannot help but sing. This is the *inward* evidence of a life that is filled with the Spirit of God.

Note where this inward evidence is manifested "in your heart" (Eph. 5:19). I am so thankful that the instrument is the heart and not the vocal chords. I often sing in my car when the windows are rolled up. I cannot make melody on an instrument. I cannot make melody with my vocal chords, but I certainly can in my heart!

To whom is this inward evidence directed? "To the Lord" (Eph. 5:19). The Holy Spirit is in the world to uplift and glorify the Lord Jesus. Music is not primarily designed by God to be a tool of evangelism. In other words, Christian music should be the result of a Spirit-filled life that is pointed to God. It is not intended for the world. It is rather unfortunate that many Christian singers today dedicate their songs to the world with the world's beat and the world's vernacular.

How is the inward evidence to be experienced? "Speaking to yourselves in psalms and hymns and spiritual songs, singing and making melody in your heart to the Lord" (Eph. 5:19, KJV). Note that it is making "melody" and not rhythm or harmony. Bill Gothard points out that rhythm appeals to the body, harmony to the soul, but melody is what appeals to the spirit. Think about it. Whichever you find predominant in music is where you will discover its intended appeal. I believe the rhythm of rock music appeals to the flesh. The sentimental harmony music appeals to the soul, the self-life. We remember such groups as the Carpenters and all the harmony, love songs. Melody is what appeals to the spirit. We make melody in our hearts to the Lord. Yes, the inward evidence of the filling of God's Holy Spirit is a song in one's heart. If one wants to know if he or she is being filled with the Spirit of God, this should be the first characteristic.

Upward Evidence

There is also an upward evidence of the filling of God's Holy Spirit. "Always giving thanks to God the Father for everything, in the name of our Lord Jesus Christ" (Eph. 5:20). Again, pay attention to whom this thanksgiving is directed—"to God" (Eph. 5:20). When we begin to recognize God as the Source of everything, and we allow His Spirit to fill us, we will commence giving thanks always for all things unto God and the Father in the name of our Lord Jesus Christ. We are to offer this upward evidence "always" (5:20).

One person chimes in, "But you don't know my problem." Another complains, "But you don't know my wife." Another says, "But you don't know my situation on the job." But the verse says, "always." We are challenged to be thankful at all times because that attitude shows that God is in control. Paul expressed it in these words, "Give thanks in all circumstances, for this is God's will for you in Christ Jesus." If we are looking for a starting point toward finding God's will, that is precisely the place to start. There is an *inward* evidence and an *upward* evidence to the filling of God's Holy Spirit.

And notice for what we are to be thankful—"everything"

(Eph. 5:20). Some are only thankful after they receive a blessing. We land a new job, and we pray, "Lord, thank you." We recover from a sickness, and we praise, "Lord, thank you." But the evidence of the filling of God's Holy Spirit is that we are thankful in *all things*. This means that we must be thankful not only after our blessings, but before a blessing, in anticipation of the victory we have awareness that it will come.

Being thankful also means we are to be thankful, not merely after and before, but even in the midst of the storms of life. Jonah certainly found this truth to be liberating when he pledged,

> "But I, with a song of thanksgiving,
>   will sacrifice to you.
>   What I have vowed I will make good.
>   Salvation comes from the Lord" (Jonah 2:9).

God appreciated that prayer of thanksgiving so much he had the fish regurgitate Jonah onto the shore. Thanksgiving, this *upward* evidence of the filling of God's Spirit, has a liberating, freeing effect. We cannot stay filled with the Holy Spirit without giving thanks always unto God for all things.

Outward Evidence

There is not only an *inward* and an *upward* evidence, but there is also an *outward* evidence of the filling of the Holy Spirit. Paul continued, "Submit to one another out of reverence for Christ" (Eph. 5:21). What is this outward evidence? It is submission. We are each to esteem the others better than ourselves. People are not sure we are filled with the Holy Spirit by our speech or the terminology we use, but the outward evidence is in our relationship with other people. Christ, of course, is our example. We remember in the upper room on the eve of His death, having instituted the Lord's Supper, how He washed His disciples' feet in a spirit of condescension. Jesus was teaching all that the greatest man is one who uses His authority to build up His people and not like the Pharisees to build themselves up. The only means of showing this outward evidence to others is by being filled with the Holy Spirit.

We are to submit to "one another." This is certainly evidence of the Spirit-filled life. Here is the solution to mountains of our problems. To solve difficulties in relationships, we must come to the knowledge of the truth about ourselves. If we are filled with the Holy Spirit we readily recognize that we have nothing to boast about. A person filled with the Holy Spirit is apt to listen and learn. The Holy Spirit helps us to realize we are members of one body, and therefore, our body functions as we submit ourselves to one another. This spirit of *unity* and *unction* is the greatest factor in church growth.

It is also intriguing to see that this outward evidence is to be performed "in the fear of God" (Eph. 5:21, KJV). This is not just some phrase tacked onto the end of a verse. We are to be submissive to one another, not because it is expedient, but because we fear God. We fear God, not so much in the sense that we fear Him by being physically afraid, but in the sense that we fear disappointing or grieving Him.

When I was in high school, I obeyed my father. My curfew was earlier than most of my high school friends. My dad always wanted to know where I was and when I was coming home. I obeyed him during those years, because I feared him, not so much that I feared him physically, but I feared disappointing him. This is what, I suppose, bothered me the most. Why should we live in submission one with another? Because of the fear of God. Could there be anything more terrifying than to realize that we were disappointing the One who loved us so much that He gave Himself for us?

The outward evidence that one is being filled with the Holy Spirit is this mutual submission—one to another. In the Ephesian letter, Paul goes on to illustrate verse 21 in three ways. The next series of verses illustrates this submission regarding the husband/wife relationship. The following verses illustrate this submission in relationship to the parent and child. And finally, to the employer and employee.

Thus, what is the proof that one is genuinely being filled with God's Holy Spirit? Is it a certain, assigned gift, or a certain terminology, or a certain miracle? No! The real proof that one is being filled with the Holy Spirit is found in the context of its command. There is an inward evidence, *a song in one's heart*. There is an upward evidence, *a spirit of thanksgiving*. And there is an outward evidence, *submitting ourselves one to another*. We will never see genuine revival until each of us comes to this element of participation, not only with others in *unity*, but with God in *unction*, the filling of God's Holy Spirit. This is the church member's most pressing need in these last days of church history.

Untold numbers of members in churches today try to give out when they have never taken in. Jesus declared, "He that believes in me as the Scripture has said, out of his belly will flow rivers of living water." There are two kinds of wells—surface wells and artesian wells. A surface well is not very deep.

When I was a small child, I used to visit my great-uncle who ran a country store nine miles outside of Pikeville, Tennessee, on the side of a mountain. I was a city boy and quite fascinated by that life-style. They had an old water pump outside the back door of their house. He would go out and pour a little water from the Mason jar into the pump, thus "priming" the pump, and then he would pump, pump, pump, until the water started flowing. As long as he pumped, it would flow, but as soon as he stopped so would the water. And one always had to remember to fill the jar, because it would have to be primed again. Have you ever known any church members like that? If you want them to serve the Lord Jesus, you have to prime the pump. So many try to enlist workers by begging and pleading and stroking. Why? Because those people are shallow like that surface well.

However, there is another kind of well that we call an artesian well. It goes down deep into the ground until it hits an underground stream or river. You don't have to pump an artesian well, all you have to do is tap into it, and it flows and flows. I hope you have known believers like that. Those church members are not complaining, "I've been here six months, and nobody has come to see me!" They are insisting, "Is there anyone I can go and visit?" These people are not carping, "No one spoke to me today!" They pick out people and make a point of speaking to them first. What is the difference? Some want to be served while others want to serve. Some are shallow, while some have tapped into the river of life and are being filled with God's Holy Spirit.

The church will be revived again when more and more of its people experience first-hand the filling of the Holy Spirit in their lives. The early church found their strength in *participation,* not only with each other, but with God: They were "all filled with the Holy Spirit."

What makes a church great in the eyes of God? The first element is vital—participation. They were all together, and they were all filled. There was unity and unction among their fellowship. They found their strength in participation with each other and participation with God. They not only had a sense of belonging to God but a sense of belonging to each other. No church will ever be a great church in the eyes of God without its membership being all together and all filled. Unity and unction are essential elements to the making of a great church in the eyes of God.

2
Proclamation

It was a beautiful, cloudless Easter morning in Fort Lauderdale, Florida, a resort city known as the "Venice of America" because of many miles of waterways within the city limits. It is also one of the most unchurched areas of the nation.

We realize that if people in this cosmopolitan and secular culture go to church at all, it is on Easter. So, one Easter we rented the large city auditorium (less threatening for the lost) and developed a massive advertising campaign to invite the city to the Easter service.

Craig came. Perhaps it was the banner he saw over Federal Highway or the gentle encouragement of his wife who had seen a newspaper advertisement and was growing desperate as she continued to watch their marriage disintegrate. Regardless, there he sat, a bit skeptical, a bit afraid that some of his "fast-lane" business associates might see him, and perhaps a bit uncomfortable having not been in church for years.

For the first time in his life, Craig heard the proclamation of the Word of God that morning. He found God's Word, as the prophet said, "like a hammer that breaks a rock to pieces." Moment by moment his hardened heart began to give way to the dynamic power of God's Word. Craig was converted that day!

Over these last few years he has served our First Baptist Church in every capacity and recently served as chairman of our deacon fellowship. He has a powerful testimony, but not nearly as powerful as his children and grandchildren who are now able to tell how they came to faith in Christ at the knee of their dad and papa.

There are so many "Craigs" in our city with so much potential for good and for God. They are hungry for the proclamation of God's Word. Deep down within, beneath all the facade, they really want to know, "What does God say about me and my life?" Real revival is always rooted and grounded in the proclamation of the Word, and when it is preached in truth and power, it leads men and women to beseech the heavens with the heartfelt cry, "Revive us again!"

[14]Then Peter stood up with the Eleven, raised his voice and addressed the crowd: "Fellow Jews and all of you who are in Jerusalem, let me explain this to you; listen carefully to what I say. [15]These men are not drunk, as you suppose. It's only nine in the morning! [16]No, this is what was spoken by the prophet Joel;

> [17]" 'In the last days, God says,
>> I will pour out my Spirit on all
>>> people.
>> Your sons and daughters will
>>> prophesy,
>>> your young men will see visions,
>>> your old men will dream dreams.

¹⁸Even on my servants, both men and
women,
I will pour out my Spirit in those
days,
and they will prophesy.
¹⁹I will show wonders in the heaven
above
and signs on the earth below,
blood and fire and billows of smoke.
²⁰The sun will be turned to darkness
and moon to blood
before the coming of the great and
glorious day of the Lord.
²¹And everyone who calls
on the name of the Lord will be
saved.'

²²"Men of Israel, listen to this: Jesus of Nazareth was a man accredited by God to you by miracles, wonders and signs, which God did among you through him, as you yourselves know. ²³This man was handed over to you by God's set purpose and foreknowledge; and you, with the help of wicked men, put him to death by nailing him to the cross. ²⁴But God raised him from the dead, freeing him from the agony of death, because it was impossible for death to keep its hold on him. ²⁵David said about him:

"'I saw the Lord always before me.
Because he is at my right hand,
I will not be shaken.
²⁶Therefore my heart is glad and my
tongue rejoices;
my body also will live in hope,

> [27]because you will not abandon me to
>   the grave,
>   nor will you let your Holy One see
>   decay.
> [28]You have made known to me the
>   paths of life;
>   you will fill me with joy in your
>   presence.'

[29]"Brothers, I can tell you confidently that the patriarch David died and was buried, and his tomb is here to this day. [30]But he was a prophet and knew that God had promised him on oath that he would place one of his descendants on his throne. [31]Seeing what was ahead, he spoke of the resurrection of the Christ, that he was not abandoned to the grave, nor did his body see decay. [32]God has raised this Jesus to life, and we are all witnesses to the fact. [33]Exalted to the right hand of God, he has received from the Father the promised Holy Spirit and has poured out what you now see and hear. [34]For David did not ascend to heaven, and yet he said,

> "'The Lord said to my Lord:
>   "Sit at my right hand
> [35]until I make your enemies
>   a footstool for your feet."'

[36]"Therefore let all Israel be assured of this: God has made this Jesus, whom you crucified, both Lord and Christ."

[37]When the people heard this, they were cut to the heart and said to Peter and the other apostles, "Brothers, what shall we do?"

³⁸Peter replied, "Repent and be baptized, every one of you, in the name of Jesus Christ so that your sins may be forgiven. And you will receive the gift of the Holy Spirit. ³⁹The promise is for you and your children and for all who are far off—for all whom the Lord our God will call."

⁴⁰With many other words he warned them; and he pleaded with them, "Save yourselves from this corrupt generation" (Acts 2:14-40).

Every believer who is halfway conversant with the New Testament will recall the transformation of Simon Peter. He preached boldly and with Pentecostal power, and the multitude was smitten by the Holy Spirit. Yes, this is the selfsame Simon Peter who denied his Lord—and cursed and lied in the process. Now Simon was bold and brassy because of the empowering of the Holy Spirit. Before this time he was outspoken and forceful in the strength of the flesh. Now he was in the anointing of the Spirit.

Can you imagine it? This was the same Simon—but not exactly. He was changed by the purging and purifying power of the Spirit.

Of the apostles, Peter was the most enthusiastic. At Caesarea Philippi, Jesus asked the apostles who people thought He was. John the Baptist? Elijah? Who? Peter, never to be outdone, answered rightly, "Thou art the Christ, the Son of the living God!"

And Jesus replied, "Simon, flesh and blood has not revealed it to you. And I say to you, you are Peter [*petros*, little stone, pebble] and upon this rock [*petra*, big rock— actually Jesus Himself and the confession that He is the Christ] will I build my church and the gates of hell will not prevail against it" (see Matt. 16:13-19). What an interchange!

And this was the man who would fight for Jesus until the end. He had boasted, "Lord, I'll never leave You. I'll stick with You." Yes, he had boasted of his faithfulness and tenacity. One time Peter thought Jesus was hinting at His own death, and blurted out, "Lord, let me go with you that I may also die." Ah, he talked a good game. He was rough and tough.

And do you recollect the time that Peter saw Jesus walking on the water? He thought to himself, *Hey, I'd like to do that too*. He was so adult and yet so immature and childish! So, he jumped out of the boat and started walking to his Lord: (1) because he wanted to walk on the water, and (2) because he wanted to be with Him. He desperately wanted to be with Jesus. But, brave Simon Peter, the "rock," saw the commotion of the waves, became afraid, and sank like a rock indeed! It was a blessing that he didn't drown—if it hadn't been for Jesus, he probably would have.

And one time Jesus spoke harsh words to Peter, "Get thee behind me, Satan." The Master was talking to Peter.

Remember when the Roman soldiers and temple guards apprehended Jesus in the garden of Gethsemane? Peter pulled a sword from beneath his clothing and impetuously whacked off Malchus's servant's ear. Jesus calmly reached out and healed the man's ear.

And who can forget the early hours of the morning when Jesus was going through a mock trial and court? Peter and all the disciples except John had run for their lives. Even though he was guilt-ridden and haunted by his denial, Peter tried to follow Jesus from afar. He no doubt remembered Jesus' rebuke. And he heard Jesus' prophetic words, "Peter, before the rooster crows three times in the morning, you will betray me!" Yet, he wanted to be near Jesus. He reminds us of a pyromaniac who often wants to watch the destructive fire he has built.

How could Peter have that kind of nerve? Somehow the people in the courtyard recognized the stamp of Jesus on Simon. "There he is. He's one of those who follows the Galilean. Yes, he ought to be arrested!" Peter kept on denying it, but they yelled, "That's him, that's him. He's a disciple of the man from Galilee." And, to reinforce his lie, Peter resorted to cursing his Lord.

Peter, you traitor! You turncoat! You Benedict Arnold! But Peter went and wept bitterly. His were tears of true repentance. Judas wept for different reasons.

After Jesus arose from the dead, one of His appearances was with Peter by the seaside. Jesus must have stung Peter by asking him three times to remind him of three denials, by saying, "Do you love Me?"

"Yes, Lord, you know that I love You," Peter said. Peter became the caretaker of the sheep, Jesus' sheep.

At Pentecost, Peter was turned inside out and transformed from a coward to a champion for Jesus Christ. Now he had been baptized, indwelt, sealed, was filled with the Holy Spirit, and anointed with power.

There will never be a church that is a great church in the eyes of God without a bold *proclamation* of the Word of God by a God-anointed and God-appointed preacher.

Gospel proclamation became the central part of the day. The preaching of the Gospel should be central in the church of the Lord Jesus Christ. It is still in this twentieth century, by the "foolishness of preaching" (or "the foolishness of the thing preached") that people are drawn to repentance. It is not simply enough to have participation; great churches are also characterized by *proclamation*.

Prophetic Preaching

Our preaching must be prophetic. In other words, it must be biblical. Peter stood up before the crowd, raised his voice, opened the scroll to the prophet Joel, and read Joel 2:28-32. He established a scriptural basis for what was happening, and for what he desired his hearers to do in response. He then illustrated his text with Psalms 16; 110. His preaching was prophetic and biblical. It is amazing that so many preachers do not seem to preach the Word of God today. A preacher who is not using the Bible would be as if a surgeon went into surgery without his scapel, because preaching the Word is what "cut to the heart" (Acts 2:37). For a preacher not to use the Word of God would be like a carpenter trying to build a home without a hammer. God spoke to us through Jeremiah saying, "Is not my word like a hammer that breaks a rock to pieces?" No wonder so many churches are empty. Our preaching must be prophetic.

The great, God-blessed churches in the world today have one common characteristic: an insistence upon an exposition of God's infallible Word. They have men behind their pulpits who select their text from the Word of God and proclaim it boldly. Peter chose a text from the prophet Joel. Joel had predicted that the Lord would come and visit His people. He prophesied that the Lord would come and live in the midst of them, and that after this supernatural visitation He would "pour out his Spirit upon all flesh." Peter asserted, "this is what was spoken by the prophet Joel" (Acts 2:16). The text was happening before their eyes.

The Bible records, "When the people heard this, they were cut to the heart" (Acts 2:37). What is it that cuts one's heart and pricks one's spirit? It is the sword, the Word of God.

The Word of God is profitable. Paul wrote to his young preacher-friend, Timothy, to remind him that "all Scripture is God-breathed and is useful for teaching, rebuking, correcting and training in righteousness, so that the man of God may be thoroughly equipped for every good work" (2 Tim. 3:16-17). The Word of God is indeed profitable. It is profitable for four things: doctrine, reproof, correction, and instruction in righteousness. An effective ministry of God's Word will do all four. It will teach doctrine, rebuke and reprove sin, correct false paths, and train and instruct in righteousness.

There are churches today that have instructed in doctrine to the virtual exclusion of instructing in righteousness or correcting false paths. These groups are dying because of their emphasis on doctrine alone.

Other churches have emphasized reproof. They feel their God-given call is continuously to speak on how long someone's hair is or how short someone's dress is. They seldom, if ever, teach doctrine or instruct in righteousness.

There are still others who have pointed out correction to the virtual exclusion of doctrine, reproof, and instruction. Like those who have stressed reproof, they are polemic and think God has called them to correct everyone else while the lost world sits by watching and quietly going to hell.

Still others have emphasized instruction in righteousness of being Holy-Spirit filled to the virtual exclusion of ever teaching doctrine. This constant emphasis on the deeper life without any strong doctrinal teaching, preaching, reproof, or correction has led to more than one division in the local body of believers.

An effective ministry of God's Word will be a balanced ministry and will do all four vital things. The Bible is profitable when it is used in a prophetic sense. As we look at Simon Peter's sermon, we find all four of these elements included. He taught doctrine as he spoke of the Deity of Christ (Acts 2:31-33,36). He reproved sin (Acts 2:23). He corrected false paths and instructed in righteousness (Acts 2:38). Peter preached a balanced, biblical, prophetic message.

First, the proclamation of the gospel must be prophetic. The only way it can be prophetic is to be biblical. What makes a church great in the eyes of God? Participation, proclamation, and preaching where the Bible proclamation is prophetic.

Plain Proclamation

Second, it must also be plain. In Acts 2:14, Peter proclaimed, "let me explain this to you; listen carefully to what I say." He was being *plain* in his approach. Peter did not make it difficult; he simply laid out the plain truth of the Word of God. He preached about sin, God's mercy in Christ, and the coming judgment, and the common people understood him. Many preachers today make their message difficult to understand. This gospel, of which we are stewards, is plain enough for a child to understand. Many churches never make an impact, because they do not preach the plain gospel. People can attend some churches for months (maybe even years) and never know what they must do to have eternal life.

The first Christian sermon was Christ-centered. Peter preached of Christ. He preached about Jesus in His incarnation, death, resurrection, and presence by His Spirit.

Peter did not preach systematic theology or philosophy, he preached Jesus: He was born to save, died on the cross, arose again, ascended, and is coming again.

Peter was *plain* in his approach. He sent the message home:

> "This man was handed over to you by God's set purpose and foreknowledge; and you, with the help of wicked men, put him to death by nailing him to the cross" (Acts 2:23).

Who crucified our Lord? The Jews? The Romans? No! I did, and you did—my sin, your sin. But in the truest sense— God did! No one took our Lord's life; He laid it down.

Peter was *plain* in the message of the gospel. The transparent truth is that the cross was no accident. Some people think the cross was some sort of last-minute band-aid on a wounded world when everything else had failed. No! A thousand times, no!

It was the program and plan of God. Peter continued in Acts 2:23: "This man was handed over to you by God's set purpose and foreknowledge." The word translated *purpose* in the *New International Version* of the Bible is the Greek word *boule*. It means God's irrevocable will, which will be done with or without our cooperation or response.[1]

There is another word, when translated, that is the English word *counsel (purpose* or *will)* which in Greek is *thelema,* simply meaning desire. We do not find that word in Acts 2:23. Instead, we discover the stronger word *boule*.

Therefore, what Peter was preaching to the crowd is this: There is nothing you could do that could have stopped or altered God's plan for the atonement of our sins at Calvary! God was in control. The Lord Jesus was handed over to you by God's "boule," God's irrevocable will, which was to be done with or without our cooperation or response. Peter's message was plain. He preached Jesus. What makes a great church? It must have the element of proclamation, which is prophetic and plain.

Positive Proclamation

Third, proclamation must also be positive. Peter continued: "God has raised this Jesus to life, and we are all witnesses of the fact" (Acts 2:32). Peter unfurled the resurrection. The resurrection should be the heart of every sermon. Our Lord is not dead. He is alive! He is here and can meet our needs today. We have a *positive* gospel!

These disciples had seen the resurrected Christ, and He had transformed their lives. Most of them met martyrs' deaths. If they had been perpetrating a lie, they would not have died for their faith. Men do not die for a lie. Peter was crucified upside-down in Rome. Being a martyr was one of the most marvelous proofs of the resurrection. Peter had seen the risen Lord. Jesus was alive! The resurrection should inject a positive note into our preaching, not some sort of superficial, pumped-up mental attitude. Every preacher should ask himself how much of his preaching points to the living Christ.

So many of our congregations today argue, "I've got to see it, and then I'll believe it."

But God says just the opposite, "You believe it, and then you'll see it."

Remember Thomas in the upper room? He struggled about this point, "I'll have to see it; then I'll believe it."

Jesus, appearing in His resurrected body, left this with him, "Thomas, blessed are those who have not seen and yet have believed." Where can we gain our positive spirit in preaching? We do not receive it from positive thinking or from possibility thinking. We should gather it from the same event Peter did, and that is the resurrection. The Lord Jesus is alive, and therefore our proclamation should be positive. There is not a need in the heart of any hearer that the living Christ cannot meet!

It was a hot, June day in Ada, Oklahoma. Early that morning I was pacing the second floor corridor at Valley View Hospital. It was a special day for our family, as our little Holly was making her grand entrance into our world. It was not long until Dr. Stevens appeared in the nursery windows and held that tiny package of love, wrapped in a pink blanket. He laid her in a bassinet and wheeled her over to the window where I could have a good look. Only a daddy can know the joy of that moment. I stood there alone for several minutes, thanking the Lord and watching that little, red-faced beauty waving her arms, kicking her feet, and crying at the top of her lungs.

Suddenly, I noticed I was no longer standing there alone. A maid with her mop bucket was looking over my shoulder. "Is that your baby?" she asked.

"Surely is," I proudly answered.

She continued, "Well, it's no wonder she's crying, being born into the world she has been born into." And then she turned around and sauntered down the hall, pushing her mop bucket before her.

For a moment I began to think, *She is right. If I believe everything I preach and teach, then it would be far better for this little girl to go on to heaven. After all, she would not have to go through all the heartaches of life and never have the haunting, longing that some moment could be lived over.*

I began to pray. It was an intimate moment with Jesus,

Holly, and me. I often pray hymns in my private devotional time, and that morning the Holy Spirit began to pray, through me, the words of a Bill Gaither hymn, "Because He Lives." When I began the second verse of the hymn, I knew I was on holy ground:

> How sweet to hold a new born baby,
> And feel the pride, and joy he gives;
> But greater still the calm assurance,
> This child can face uncertain days
>   because he lives.
>
> Because he lives I can face tomorrow;
> Because he lives, all fear is gone;
> Because I know he holds the future,
> And life is worth the living
>   just because he lives.[2]

What makes a church great in the eyes of God? It is not only made up of participation, but also *proclamation*. And our proclamation must be *prophetic, plain,* and *positive*.

Personal Proclamation

Fourth, proclamation must also be personal. Although Peter was preaching to a multitude of people, he was preaching on a personal level. Hear him as he says, "This man was handed over to *you* by God's set purpose and fore-knowledge; and *you,* with the help of wicked men, put *him* to death by nailing *him* to the cross" (Acts 2:23, author's italics). Note the personal pronouns. Preaching today is mostly in the first person plural or the third person plural. That is, we are to use a lot of *we* and *they* in our preaching. This type of preaching seldom brings about conviction.

Peter preached in second person, saying, "You, with the help of wicked men, put him to death by nailing him to the cross." You, you, you!

There are many preachers today who are afraid of offending deacons, elders, vestrymen, big givers, this person or that person, that civic leader or politician. It is no wonder many churches today have such little power. Our proclamation should be personal. I believe there is not much personal preaching together. Peter's preaching was not aimed just at the head but also at the heart. It was personal, and when he finished, the Bible reports, "When the people heard this, they were cut to the heart" (Acts 2:37).

What makes a church great in the eyes of God? The element of proclamation is vital. This proclamation must not only be *prophetic, plain,* and *positive,* it must also be *personal.*

Penetrating Proclamation

Fifth, it must also be penetrating. Acts 2:37 tells us, "When the people heard this, they were cut to the heart and said to Peter and the other apostles, 'Brothers, what shall we do?'" What happened? The Word testifies that the people's hearts were "cut." We have a word for that; we call it conviction. Much modern preaching is superficial, designed to make the hearers feel good. I have heard preachers in some churches even boast that people can come to their services and never feel guilty about their life-styles. They advertise that they are there to "make you feel good." Well, Peter's sermon "cut his hearers to the heart." The truth is, the only way we'll ever feel good about ourselves is to see ourselves for who we are, to confess that our sin put Christ on the cross. Once we realize this and are set free through the blood of Jesus Christ, we will have the best feeling we've ever had. Then we'll be able to sing:

> Free from the law, Oh happy condition
> Jesus bled and there is remission
> Cursed by the fall, condemned by the law
> Christ has redeemed us, once for all.

Lyrics by P. P. BLISS

Until a person sees that there is no hope within himself to satisfy the righteous demands of the law, the cross is simply a farce to him. When conviction of sin arrives, we are aware that the only way we can get right with God is through the cross of our Lord Jesus Christ. Some people have never felt conviction. Their hearts have never been cut. Why? Because in too many cases they have not been under the preaching of the gospel which is prophetic, plain, positive, and personal.

When these men and women at Pentecost realized what they had done in crucifying the Lord Jesus Christ, their hearts were broken. Why aren't more people's hearts cut in our churches today? It is because they do not realize that they ought to assume personal responsibility for their sin. And why? Because there is not enough preaching today which is penetrating. There are few preachers who even mention sin today. Sin is often the forgotten word in the pulpit today. No wonder many churches are dead and dying. There is no conviction in them, and without conviction there can be no conversion!

Conviction always precedes conversion. These people were "cut to the heart." This was a recognition of sin. Here is a broken and contrite heart. This process is called spiritual birth, and it is pictured in physical birth. There must be birth pains before the child is born, and so it is in spiritual birth. We cannot experience the new birth without godly sorrow over sin any more than one can give natural childbirth without experiencing birth pains. Conviction leads to conversion.[3] A host of people make some sort of "decision" early in life but have never really realized that they have personally sinned and put Christ on the cross. They were never really "cut to the heart" because of their sin.

Here we find the first account of the convicting work of the Holy Spirit. Jesus had prophesied the night before the crucifixion,

> "But I tell you the truth: It is for your good that I am going away. Unless I go away, the Counselor will not come to you; But if I go, I will send him to you. When he comes, he will convict the world of guilt in regard to sin and righteousness and judgment: in regard to sin, because men do not believe in me" (John 16:7-9).

While in my first pastorate at Hobart, Oklahoma, I learned a lot from those southwestern Oklahoma wheat farmers. In fact, I learned more from those dear, old men who had spent a lifetime in the Book of God than I did from some of my professors. Being a city boy, I was fascinated by farm life. I learned there were several things necessary in order to grow a good crop.

First, the ground had to be broken. Farmers would use their tractors and plows and turn the sod over and over, breaking up the dirt. Second, the seed had to be planted. Third, the wheat was cultivated, watered, and nurtured.

Finally, about the first of June every year, the harvest was gathered!

Many churches today wonder why they never reap a harvest. Perhaps they have never broken ground! The Word of God cuts to the heart, and often there is not a great deal of preaching regarding the Word of God. Our preaching must be penetrating. We will never see the harvest if we do not preach the Word of God. It doesn't matter whether the seed is planted or whether the ground is cultivated, if it is not first broken, there will be no harvest.

What makes a church great? The element of participation and the element of proclamation. Our proclamation should be *prophetic, plain, personal,* and *penetrating*.

Persuasive Proclamation

Sixth, it must also be persuasive. Acts 2:37 says, "When the people heard this, they were cut to the heart and said to Peter and the other apostles, 'Brothers, what shall we do?'" God-anointed preaching is *persuasive* preaching. It goes straight to the heart, and people begin to ask what was asked in this text, "What shall we do?" What a burning question! One who is convicted does not know what to do. It is not in the natural man's heart. It is "not by works of righteousness which we have done, but according to his mercy he has saved us" (Titus 3:5, KJV).

Much preaching today falls on deaf ears, and often it is not the hearer's fault. At least many hearers are there, in their place and in their pew. Much of the preaching today is not persuasive, because in place of being plain it is complicated; in place of being positive it is critical; in place of being personal it is courteous, so as not to offend; and in place of being penetrating it is often cosmetic. No wonder modern preaching is not leading more people to ask, "What shall we do?"

What shall we do? This is the basic question we must ask in the twentieth-century church, almost the twenty-first if Jesus tarries. What shall we do? It is not enough to be sorry for our sin. What shall we do? The question has a real ring of desperation in it. What shall we do? It is like the Philippian jailer who asked, "'What must I do to be saved?'" (Acts 16:30).

On the Day of Pentecost the hearers were "cut to the heart" (Acts 2:37). Note when they asked the question, "What shall we do?" it was when they heard Peter say in the previous verse, "God has made this Jesus whom you crucified both Lord and Christ." Jesus is Lord! He is risen from the dead, and He is Lord. This confronts us all with the question, "What shall we do?" What shall we do about the Lordship of Jesus Christ? Josh McDowell says he is either Lord or liar, and our eternal destiny hinges upon what we believe about this fact.

If the church in America today had sufficient power, today's masses, as the crowd did at Pentecost, would first be asking, "'What does this mean?'" (Acts 2:12). Then they would be asking, "'What shall we do?'" (Acts 2:37). Our proclamation must be persuasive.

Pointed Proclamation

Seventh, it must also be pointed. Peter answered their question with a pointed reply by saying, "repent" (Acts 2:38). He commanded his hearers what they ought to do. He did not give them several multiple-choice options. He was pointed. In a word he replied, "repent." What shall we do?

Repent. Much preaching today is so vague. People can sit in some churches for months without any idea of how to apply the message to their lives on Monday through Friday. Preaching must not only be prophetic, it must be *pointed*.

Peter's pointed proclamation was a word—*repent*. There are three pertinent questions to be asked at this point: *What is repentance? Why is repentance important? And where is repentance found in the salvation process?*

First, what is repentance? There seems to be considerable confusion regarding what repentance is. Let's look first at what repentance is *not*. Repentance is not *remorse*. It is not simply being sorry for our sin. Remorse may lead to repentance, but remorse is not repentance. The rich, young ruler went away very sorrowful when Jesus explained the demands of discipleship. He was remorseful, but he did not repent. Many people have substituted remorse for repentance.

Repentance is not *regret*. That is, it is not merely wishing some sinful deed, word, or action had not occurred. Pontius Pilate ceremonially took a basin of water and washed his hands, regretting his evil deed, but he did not repent. Many people substitute regret for repentance and tragically fool themselves in the process.

Repentance is not *resolve*. All of us have made New Year's resolutions. Many of us resolve to assume a new set of moral standards and live life on a higher plane but never seem able to turn that "new leaf over" for any considerable period of time. We cannot substitute resolve for repentance.

It is not enough to sing "I Am Resolved," unless that is coupled with "godly sorrow," unless the repentance is genuine within one's heart, and unless there is a determination wrought by the Holy Spirit, in which one never wants to sin again, even though such is impossible here. But there must be that determination none-the-less. Genuine repentance is characterized by the person's saying to himself and God, "I never want to displease the Lord again. I am so sorry for my sins. I am leaving that old life behind me. I don't want to be the same. I want to be changed by the Holy Spirit."

Through the years, I have heard more people make resolves that they have never followed. They bargained with the Lord, "O, Lord, if you just get me out of this mess, I'll do whatever You want. I'll follow wherever you lead. Lord, just help me." And the Lord does help them; they get out of their jam. And what happens? They go on living as they did before, making a mockery out of God, ignoring Him, and never looking back to those resolutions, because they were not accompanied by real repentance and doing a right about-face from sin. A mere resolution will not suffice.

Repentance is not *reform*. Sometimes reformation even involves restitution. It was so with Judas Iscariot. After betraying our Lord, he grabbed the thirty pieces of silver, returned to the temple and threw it at those who had paid the price of betrayal. Judas reformed, but unfortunately he did not repent. Many people today have substituted reform for repentance. Peter did not preach on the Day of Pentecost and say, "Reform." Nor did he say, "Resolve." Nor did he say, "Regret." Nor did he say, "Have remorse." His message was a pointed call for repentance.[4]

We have seen what repentance is not; now let us examine what repentance is. Is repentance turning from every sin as some people preach today? If so, then who has repented? When you came to Christ, did you turn from every sin you had ever committed? The truth is, in our natural state we are spiritually dead, not sick, and therefore unresponsive to the gospel. The Bible reminds us: "The natural man receiveth not the things of the Spirit of God: for they are foolishness to him: neither can he know them, because they are spiritually discerned" (1 Cor. 2:14, KJV). What is repentance? The word *repent* is the Greek word *metanoeo,* which in its original language is defined as a change of mind.[5] It is to change one's way of thinking about salvation. Repentance makes you love what you once hated, and hate what you once loved. When I was converted at age seventeen, I had never heard the word *repentance*. In fact, it was some weeks or perhaps months after my conversion before I ever remember hearing the word. But I know I repented! How do I know? The bad things I used to love, I no longer desired, and the things I never thought I would like became the things I loved to do. It was a change of mind.

Repentance is a change of mind. Repentance involves a change of your mind about yourself, a change of your mind about sin, and a change of your mind about salvation. It is a change of mind that is always evidenced in three areas.

First, *attitude* is changed—that is, intellectually. As stated, it is a change of mind. This is where we begin. This is repentance.

Second, there is a change in the *affections*—the heart. If one genuinely changes one's mind, then a change of heart will follow.

The third result of a change of mind is a change in *action*. There will be a change in one's will or volition. If we genuinely changed our minds, our hearts will be changed, and if our hearts have been changed, a change in our will will follow. Paul said, "Therefore, if anyone is in Christ, he is a new creation; the old has gone, the new has come!" (2 Cor. 5:17). If we have experienced salvation our lives will be altered. We will no longer look at life, ourselves, and others as we once did. Like the prodigal son, God will give us new wishes and desires. This is repentance!

Since repentance is a change of mind, a person may be moved to tears emotionally by a sermon, and one's heart may overflow with remorse or regret, but it is not necessarily repentance. A person may have one's will manipulated by various means, but if he or she has not repented (changed one's mind), he or she is not saved. Jesus made it clear, "Except ye repent, ye shall all likewise perish" (Luke 13:3, KJV).

We find our most obvious biblical illustration of repentance in Luke 15 with the story of the prodigal son. Here was a young man who had gone to a far country and wasted all of his inheritance on ungodly living. He was far away from home. First of all, this boy came to have *a change of attitude*. Luke 15:17 (KJV) notes "he came to himself"—that is, he changed his mind. Then what happened? He had *a change of affection*. He thought to himself,

"How many hired servants have bread enough and to spare, and I am perishing with hunger!

I will arise and go to my father, and will say unto him, Father, I have sinned against heaven, and before thee,

And am no longer worthy to be called thy son" (Luke 15:17-19, KJV).

His heart was changed. Then what happened after his change of mind resulted in a changed heart? He had *a change of action;* his will was changed, and so was his direction. "I will arise and go to my father." And Luke 15:20 states: "He got up and went to his father."

The prodigal son had a change of mind. That was repentance. It was evident in four areas. He regretted his deed; he blamed himself for his sin; he acknowledged his father's right to be displeased, as he felt he was no longer worthy to be called his father's son; and he resolved to sin no more. After this, he went home. Repentance is a change of mind. The battle is in the mind, and the proof is in these four areas. Each of us will repent when we change our minds, and in changing our minds, our hearts will be changed. Therefore, a change in our will and volition will follow. This change of mind will cause us to regret our deed and blame ourselves for it, take responsibility for the deed, and resolve to set our face toward the Lord Jesus Christ.

By now it should be apparent why repentance is important. To begin with, it was the message of the Old Testament prophets, who were all preachers of repentance. As far back as Noah, we hear them calling on the people to forsake their wicked ways and turn to the Lord.

It was the message of the forerunner John the Baptist: "Repent, for the kingdom of heaven is near" (Matt. 3:2). And Matthew 3:7-8 says, "But when he saw many of the Pharisees and Sadducees coming to where he was baptizing, he said to them; 'You brood of vipers! Who warned you to flee from the coming wrath? Produce fruit in keeping with repentance.'"

Let's face it. I doubt if John the Baptist could make it as a pastor in most churches today. His preaching was pointed. He preached without fear or favor. He laid the ax to the tree. He didn't care who it offended, if God laid the message on his heart.

John the Baptist denounced Herod for adultery. He referred to his listeners as vipers and snakes. How long would a preacher last, if he called his listeners snakes, unless he

were preaching to real snakes—the kind that slither and
have forked tongues? And what kind of response did he
receive? Well, the common people rejoiced over his straight-
forward ministry. However, the folks at the palace didn't
like him. Herodias asked Herod for John's (decapitated)
head on a platter in exchange for an exotic dance from Sa-
lome. John the Baptist was imprisoned and then beheaded
for preaching the truth pointedly.

It was the message of the Lord Jesus Himself. He com-
menced His ministry with the message of repentance. The
Bible reports, "From that time on Jesus began to preach
'Repent, for the kingdom of heaven is near'" (Matt. 4:17).
And in Mark 1:14-15:

> After John was put in prison, Jesus went into Galilee, pro-
> claiming the good news of God. "The time has come," he
> said. "The kingdom of God is near. Repent and believe the
> good news!"

Jesus continued His ministry with the message of repentance by saying, "I tell you, no! But unless you repent, you
too will all perish" (Luke 13:3). The burden of His heart was
in a word—*repent.* Jesus concluded His ministry with the
word *repentance* as recorded in Luke 24:46-47:

> He told them, "This is what is written: The Christ will suf-
> fer and rise from the dead on the third day, and repentance
> and forgiveness of sins will be preached in his name in all
> nations."

One of the greatest books on evangelism that I have ever
read is *With Christ After the Lost* by L. R. Scarborough,
former president of Southwestern Baptist Theological Seminary. Let me share a few of his words with you:

The Winning Characteristics of Jesus' Preaching

1. Its simplicity, utilizing everyday illustrations, simple but pungent words,
2. Its positiveness and divine authority,
3. Its heart-searching, bone-breaking, conviction-bringing power,
4. Its richness and abundance of fundamental doctrine and principles,
5. Its supreme tenderness and love, often mingled with scathing, blistering denunciation,
6. Its direct and personal reach,
7. Its unfailing appeal to the highest in man and God.[6]

Jesus' first sermon was "Repent and believe the good news." It was also the message of the Great Commission. In Matthew's account of this, God gives us the mechanics. We are to *make* disciples, *mark* disciples by baptism, and *mature* disciples by teaching them to observe the faith. These are the *mechanics* of the Great Commission, and Mark's account gives us the *measure* of it.

We are commanded to take the gospel to the whole world. And in Luke's account of the Commission, he gave us the message of the Great Commission. What is it? "That repentance and remission of sins should be preached . . . among all nations" (Luke 24:47, KJV). Jesus *commenced, continued,* and *concluded* His ministry with the same word—repent. How can a minister today claim to be preaching the gospel of Jesus Christ if he leaves out the heart of our Lord's message? *Our preaching must be pointed.*

It was also the message of the apostles. "They went out and preached that people should repent" (Mark 6:12). They went out and preached. What did they preach? Prosperity?

Successful living? What? They went out and preached that people should repent.

It was the message of Simon Peter. Hear him at Pentecost, raising his voice in his mighty sermon, and answering the question of what the people should do with a one-word reply—"Repent!"

Scarborough summed up the characteristics of Simon Peter:

> But Peter's greatest distinction is that he was the Evangelist of Pentecost. His voice and ministry introduced the age and ministry of the Holy Ghost. John the Baptist introduced Jesus, and Peter introduced the Holy Spirit to a lost world. He preached the first sermon in the world under the vice-regency of the Divine Spirit after Christ's ascension.[7]

Scarborough continued concerning Peter:

1. His simple straightforwardness of character and manner . . . He had no dignity to bother him. He was hampered by no sacred traditions. He struck straight. Dignities, ministerial stiffness, conventionalities and all such hinder; Gospel evangelism and the true approach to souls. Peter went after lost men like he sought the finny tribe of stormy Galilee—cast his net in where the fish were and pulled them into his boat.
2. He preached plain, unvarnished truth right out without apology or compromise. He saw men as sinners and realized their need was Christ and knew that the Gospel revealed Christ to them. He threw a hot Gospel at the bared souls of men in great golden chunks. His sermon on the Day of Pentecost is packed with doctrine . . . He did not mince matters. He dodged nothing.[8]

It was the message of the apostle Paul. Hear him: " 'In the past God overlooked such ignorance, but now he commands all people everywhere to repent' " (Acts 17:30). Hear him later: "I have declared to both Jews and Greeks that they must turn to God in repentance and have faith in our Lord Jesus" (Acts 20:21).

Elements in Paul of Soul-winning Success

1. A fourfold vision. (1) He saw himself a lost, ruined sinner, dead in trespasses and sin, without God, hope and Christ in the world. (2) He saw Christ and His Gospel as God's dynamic power to save to the uttermost (Rom. 1:16). (3) He realized the lordship and mastery of the conquering Christ, whose every order must be obeyed and every purpose fulfilled. (4) He saw the vision of a world ruined by sin and heard its inmost and deepest soul-cry for spiritual help. He yielded his life to such a service. He said, "I was not disobedient to the heavenly vision" (Acts 26:19).

2. His holy courage, fearing only God's disfavor . . .

3. A victorious, reliant, restful faith. . . .

4. A holy optimism based on predestination's securities and Christ's unfailing promises.

5. A consuming love for Jesus Christ and a deathless compassion for lost men (2 Cor. 5:14; Rom. 9:1-3).

6. A mighty relentless heart-grip on the vitals of the truth. . . .

7. Versatility and adaptability of method. . . .

8. One of his chief marks of success was his holy and consecrated life. . . .

9. Above all he was a man full of the Holy Spirit who built all his ministry around the crucified, risen Christ. . . .[9]

It was the message of John the beloved apostle. Simply turn to the message directed to the churches of Asia, as recorded in the early chapters of Revelation, and discover that eight times, in letters to the seven churches, he pealed forth the message of repentance. Why is it important? Because it is the message of the Bible.

What was the message of the Bible? What was the message of the early church? Was it positive thinking, with all sorts of trinkets for reminders? Was it concentrated ministries on the home, ministries on finance, or selected other "professional ministries"? When we read the Book of Acts, we find none of these in the early church. Why? Their message was "repent."

This is what accounts for a happy home—when a husband and wife repent. We can fill out workbooks until we are blue in the face and sit before videotaped seminars until we can sit no longer (and some of those are good), but I believe what the church severely needs today is the message of repentance. When a person genuinely repents, he or she will put one's home in order.

It is strange how many preachers are silent today concerning the message of repentance. It could be that some have lost sight of the sinfulness of mankind. Today some are preaching who deny the Bible truth of a literal, burning hell, or at least they never mention it. There are many preachers today who hold the doctrine of universalism, believing that ultimately and eventually everyone will be saved. Consequently, what need is there for the message of repentance in these churches? Too many churches and preachers have lost sight of the lostness of humankind and the holiness of God. Perhaps it is because repentance is not a popular message. Of course, it is indeed more popular to "tickle the ears" of our listeners with messages of comfort, sweetness, and light.

This presents another question: Where is repentance in salvation? What did Peter mean in this Pentecostal sermon? Does repentance precede faith? Or does faith precede repentance? Think about it. Does one repent before one can exercise faith? If you believe repentance is turning from every sin, then faith must come first, because repentance would then become a work of salvation. This is the idea of some today.

But if repentance is turning from every sin, then who has repented? Conversely, if you believe that repentance is indeed a change of mind, then repentance is first in the order, because a person must change one's way of thinking before he or she can grasp the free promise, the grace of God in Christ Jesus. Now, since humankind is totally depraved and since God sovereignly calls us unto Himself, it stands to reason that God, then, must grant repentance to us, because we cannot obtain it in our own depraved condition.

This is exactly what the Bible teaches. Take for example 2 Timothy 2:24-25:

> And the Lord's servant must not quarrel; instead, he must be kind to everyone, able to teach, not resentful. Those who oppose him he must gently instruct, in the hope that God will grant them repentance leading them to a knowledge of the truth.

Repentance is the gift of God's grace that transforms the mind. God grants unto us repentance. When the attitude is genuinely transformed, the heart is transformed, and this effects a change of action. Faith and repentance are as much the gifts of God as the Savior upon whom our faith rests. Salvation is from first to last, all of grace. Listen to Acts 5:31: "God exalted him to his own right hand as Prince and Savior that he might *give repentance* and forgiveness of sins to Israel" (author's italics). The truth is our Lord Jesus has gone up so that grace might come down. Repentance is the gift of God given to us by Christ.

There is a positive motive that produces repentance. It is not so much the message of "bumper-sticker evangelism" which might read, "turn or burn." It is more the message found in the Roman letter where Paul says, "God's kindness [goodness] leads you toward repentance" (Rom. 2:4).

We are so privileged to hear the gospel: The gospel which millions (perhaps billions) of people on our planet have never heard. We are privileged to take the message of repentance. Today, missionaries' feet have never before walked in so many little villages. A copy of God's Word has not been translated into the dialects and languages of some, and they die in the darkness; millions going down. And us? We are placed in the very spotlight of the Christian life. And yet, few of us have any time for the Lord Jesus. Can't we understand that it is the goodness of God which allows us to hear the gospel and that this is what leads us to repentance? Peter stood up and shouted, "Repent!"

The Bible does not indicate that it is the kindness of God that *calls* us to repentance, but it says, "the kindness of God *leads* us to repentance." The truth is God calls us to repentance by the gospel, but God leads us to repentance by His goodness. The goodness of God comes to us where we are; takes us by the hand, as though we were a little child; and leads us to repentance. The goodness of God leads us to repentance.

His amazing grace is offered freely through His goodness and mercy. He guides and leads the unconverted person toward repentance, God, faith, and our Lord Jesus Christ (Acts 21:20). Many are the questions which frail humans raise.

Doubters and others who have grown bitter remind me of an illustration I heard years ago. You see, the goodness, kindness, and love of God are like the sun. We could compare the heart to butter or mud. When the sun beats down on the butter, it melts. When the sun shines on the mud, it turns hard like brick. This is the nature of the human heart.

When the convicting Son of God shines upon some hearts, they melt like butter. When He beams upon other hearts, they turn to hardened brick. Only the goodness of God can lead us to repentance, and men and women must let Him do His work of repentance.

My family and I spend vacations in a quaint little village in the Great Smoky Mountains known as Maggie Valley. It is a refreshing retreat, far from the massive traffic jams and bustle of Fort Lauderdale. It is like stepping into a time tunnel; there are sights and sounds that we never see and hear in our metropolis.

One summer, when our girls were small, we rented an old, white farmhouse on the side of a mountain. It was a lovely spot, but a little scary for our two small, city girls. The children slept upstairs, and the whole house creaked whenever anyone took a step. The first night happened to be one of those pitch-black summer nights in the mountains. As James Weldon Johnson described in *God's Trombones,* "It was blacker than a hundred midnights down in a cypress swamp."

I was awakened in the middle of the night by the cries of our youngest daughter, who was only six or seven years old at the time. I bounded up the stairs to find her standing in the dark, calling for me. Taking her by the hand, I led her down the steps into the security of my bed where she slept soundly for the rest of the night. And so, our dear Heavenly Father finds us in the dark and takes us by the hand. The Bible gives a comforting word, "He leads us to repentance." When these men and women at Pentecost asked, "What shall we do?" Peter's reply came quickly. "Repent!" What should we do in our twentieth-century world? The Bible answers us plainly and clearly. Repent! Change your mind. Turn around. Go in a different direction.

So what is the message the church should be preaching today? Repentance. Peter was preaching: "You have missed God's offer of salvation. You are missing the purpose for which you were created."

What can you do about it? Change your mind![10] Change your mind about your sin. Change your mind about the Lord Jesus Christ. Change your mind about yourself. Change your mind about the plan of salvation. Note Peter's promise is that they would receive forgiveness. He did not promise them wind, fire, or tongues. The important aspect here is forgiveness of sin.

Note the conclusion of Acts 2:38: "Repent and be baptized, every one of you, in the name of Jesus Christ so that your sins may be forgiven. And you will receive the gift of the Holy Spirit." Repent and what? Repent and be baptized!

There is tremendous confusion and controversy over this verse today—in fact, for centuries. Does this mean we must be baptized in order to have our sins removed? Some answer with an emphatic yes. It certainly appears so by this verse. But what does the Bible really mean here?

The key is found in the preposition, translated in English as *for*. It is the Greek word *eis*. This same Greek word is translated two ways in the English Bible. In some verses it is translated *for* or *in order to,* and in other verses as *because of*.[11] Now the same word is used in both instances. The meaning in Acts 2:38 is not *in order to* but *because of*. Think for a moment. Just with our English vernacular, we say, "He was electrocuted *for murder*." Does that mean *in order to* or *because of*? Or take for example the statement, "He has been rewarded for good grades."[12] Do we mean *in order to* or *because of*? Listen again to Acts 2:38: "Repent and be baptized, every one of you, in the name of Jesus Christ so that your sins may be forgiven." What do you think it means? Be baptized in order to have your sins forgiven or be baptized because your sins are forgiven?

It becomes even more plain when we look into the Greek New Testament. For example, look at Matthew 12:41, where the same Greek word *eis* is translated *at*. "The men of Ninevah will stand up at the judgment with this generation and condemn it; for they repented *at* the preaching of Jonah, and now one greater than Jonah is here." The word *at* here is the Greek word *eis*. It is the same Greek word we find in Acts 2:38. The Ninevites repented *because of* the preaching of Jonah. I believe that the proper translation of the word *eis* is *because of*. Acts 2:38 can well and properly be translated, "Repent and be baptized *because of* the forgiveness of your sins." We should be baptized because our sins are forgiven, and it is an outward expression of the inward experience. We *are not* baptized because water will wash away a single sin and merit salvation for us.

Some claim that the phrase in Acts 2:38, "Be baptized, every one of you, in the name of Jesus Christ," is parenthetical. Those who adhere to this view do so from a grammatical viewpoint in the Greek. For example, the verb *repent* is plural and so is the pronoun *your*.[13] The imperative "be baptized" is singular. It is set off from the rest of the sentence in a parenthetical sort of way. Therefore, read the verse like this: "Repent for the forgiveness of your sins." This certainly fits with what the same preacher, Simon Peter, emphasized later in Acts 10:43: "All the prophets testify about him that everyone who believes in him receives forgiveness of sins through his name." This same expression, "sins may be forgiven," is found in its use here at Caesarea. There is no mention here at Cornelius's house of baptism for salvation, although they were all baptized as a confession of their faith because their sins had been forgiven.

Whatever Peter meant in Acts 2:38, it must be understood that nowhere do the Scriptures teach that salvation is dependent upon water baptism. Twice in the Corinthian letter Paul states clearly what the gospel is, and baptism is certainly not included.

In 1 Corinthians 1:17, he wrote, "For Christ did not send me to baptize, but to preach the gospel—not with words of human wisdom, lest the cross of Christ be emptied of its power."

In 1 Corinthians 15:1-4, he penned these lines,

> Now, brothers, I want to remind you of the gospel I preached to you, which you received and on which you have taken your stand. By this gospel you are saved, if you hold

firmly to the word I preached to you. Otherwise, you have believed in vain.

For what I received I passed on to you as of first importance: that Christ died for our sins according to the Scriptures, that he was buried, that he was raised on the third day according to the Scriptures.

God-anointed preaching produces *conviction*. This leads to *conversion* and then to *confession*. This is the order. It begins with conviction (Acts 2:37), which leads to conversion and results in confession (Acts 2:38). Baptism is vitally important, not for conversion but for confession. It signifies outwardly what has occurred inwardly. Our preaching must be pointed. It must tell people what the text says and what it wants them to do. The Christian's primary desire should always be to win people to repentance toward God and faith in the Lord Jesus Christ. And what makes a great church in the eyes of God? There has never been a great church in the eyes of God that didn't make much of a proclamation that was prophetic, plain, positive, personal, penetrating, persuasive, and pointed.

Pious Proclamation

Eighth, it must also be pious. By pious we mean "God fearing." We are not talking about pious in the sense of its modern connotation, but pious in the sense that we fear God and realize that He is the sovereign Lord. That is what Peter meant when he used the phrase "all whom the Lord our God will call" (Acts 2:39). Our proclamation must be pious. Great preachers and teachers realize that God is sovereign and that He is the one who adds to the church; thus they have a real sense of dependence upon Him and a deeper desire to be faithful to His Word in life and lip.

Acts 2:39 is a key to understanding this vital principle. "The promise is for you and your children and for all who are far off—for all whom the Lord our God will call." The promise is for all whom our Lord God will call. There are two types of calls—the outward call and the inward call. Peter gave the outward call, but do you know who was saved that day? Not everyone there was saved. In fact, the Bible tells us that some of them mocked him. The ones who were saved that day were "all whom the Lord God called." Our proclamation must be pious in that we realize our job is faithfulness to the outward call and trust in the Lord Jesus by His Spirit to issue the inward call.

Through the years many people who have rejected the Lord have alibied to me, "Well, preacher, I just don't want to become a Christian now, but I will later, when I feel like the time is right." I have pointed out that you can't come to Jesus at your convenience. It has to be in *His time*. It must be when He calls.

This is why evangelists like Billy Graham have preached, in essence, so many times, "If you have the slightest impulse to come to Jesus Christ, do it now, because God has put that call into your heart. It may not come tomorrow."

"Now is the accepted time; behold, now is the day of salvation" (2 Cor. 6:2, KJV). That means the day of salvation is when God gives that inward call. I repeat: You just can't come to Jesus when you please. For you to be truly saved, the Holy Spirit must be dealing with your heart. You must be under conviction.

In many churches today, the conviction of the Holy Spirit is never preached. Where there is no conviction, there can

be no salvation. The apostle John in his Gospel quoted
Jesus Himself as He prepared the apostles for His crucifixion, resurrection, and His ascension.

> I will not leave you comfortless: I will come to you (14:18,
> KJV).

> And when he [Holy Spirit] is come, he will reprove the
> world of sin, and of righteousness, and of judgment:
> Of sin, because they believe not on me,
> Of righteousness, because I go to my Father, and ye see
> me no more;
> Of judgment, because the prince of this world is judged"
> (16:8-11, KJV).

Who does the convicting? The Holy Spirit. Who does the
convincing and converting? The Holy Spirit. And without
convicting power working in one's life, you can never be
saved.

As you read the lines, and you sense that you are un-
saved, hope with all of your heart that you will fall under
conviction, that you will see your sins that have sent Jesus
to the cross, and that you will see yourself as God presently
sees you—undone, condemned, lost, but also as precious in
His sight. Long for the conviction that will lead to your repentance and faith.

Consider the following words of our Lord at this very
point:

> "All that the Father gives me will come to me, and who-
> ever comes to me I will never drive away" (John 6:37).

> "No one can come to me unless the Father who sent me
> draws him, and I will raise him up at the last day" (John
> 6:44).

Do you remember Jesus' declaration to Simon Peter after
Peter's great confession at Caesarea Philippi? "'Blessed
are you, Simon son of Jonah, for this was not revealed to
you by man, but by my Father in heaven'" (Matt. 16:17).
Paul put it like this:

> Because those who are led by the Spirit of God are sons of
> God (Rom. 8:14).

> But when God, who set me apart from birth and called me
> by his grace, was pleased (Gal. 1:15).

Peter declared,

> But you are a chosen people, a royal priesthood, a holy na-
> tion, a people belonging to God, that you may declare the
> praises of him who called you out of darkness into his won-
> derful light (1 Pet. 2:9).

> And the God of all grace, who called you to his eternal glory
> in Christ, after you have suffered a little while, will him-
> self restore you and make you strong, firm and steadfast
> (1 Pet. 5:10).

How can two people sit on the same pew in the same worship service, sing the same songs, hear the same sermon
with the same anointing, and one of them feel absolutely no
need of coming to Christ—or anything spiritual for that
matter—in his heart, and the other fall under deep conviction of sin and a longing to know Jesus personally?
How can this happen? It happens by the inward call of
God.

The most obvious Scripture illustration of this point is
found in Acts 16, when Paul was preaching at the riverside
near Philippi. The Bible records,

One of those listening was a woman named Lydia, a dealer in purple cloth from the city of Thyatira, who was a worshiper of God. *The Lord opened her heart* to respond to Paul's message (Acts 16:14, author's italics).

Paul issued the outward call, and the Lord spoke to Lydia's heart, issuing the inward call.

There are a few extremists today who have carried these doctrines of grace to the point of perverting the Scripture by denying the free offer of the gospel, and in so doing have set their camps dangerously close to the border of heresy. The fact that salvation is God's work, and He takes the initiative in calling us, does not diminish one's intensity in preaching the gospel to every creature and sharing the outward call to every last person on this planet. We have a Great Commission to "preach the gospel to every creature" (Mark 16:15, KJV). This is why doctrines of grace should intensify our evangelistic efforts. We are to proclaim to the world the outward call and then trust the Holy Spirit to issue the inward call. Here again is this element of the participation of God in the call of the gospel.

To the person who literally believes in the Great Commission, it is inconceivable that any blood-bought Christian could make rationalizations like these:

> God's going to save people when He pleases, without any help of mine or yours.

> I can't go because God's not ready for me yet.

> If God's going to save the heathen, He'll do it Himself without our interference.

We cannot comprehend it, but God has chosen frail, faulted people like you and me to be His messenger boys and girls. Jesus declared in John 20:21: "As my Father hath sent me, even so send I you" (KJV). And what was Jesus sent to do? "For the Son of man is come to seek and to save that which was lost" (Luke 19:10, KJV). We cannot save them, but we are to seek them. God has called on us to extend the outward call. He does the inward work. We do the outward call under the leadership of the Holy Spirit.

The last invitation of the Bible says,

> The Spirit and the bride say, "Come!" And let him who hears say, "Come!" Whoever is thirsty, let him come; and whoever wishes, let him take the free gift of the water of life (Rev. 22:17).

Here we see the outward call and the inward call. The bride (the church of Jesus Christ) says come—this is the outward call. But there is also the inward call—the Spirit says come. What makes a great church? It must be a church that proclaims the Word of God in a sense that is totally dependent upon the Holy Spirit.

> Rescue the perishing,
>   Care for the dying,
> Snatch them in pity
>   from sin and the grave;
> Weep o'er the erring one,
>   Lift up the fallen,
> Tell them of Jesus
>   the mighty to save.
> Rescue the perishing, Care for the dying;
>   Jesus is merciful, Jesus will save.[14]

> Lyrics by FANNIE J. CROSBY

Persistent Proclamation

Ninth, it must also be persistent. The Bible says, "With many other words . . . he pleaded with them" (Acts 2:40). The English word translated *pleading* or *exhorting* is the word *parakeleo*. It means to beseech with strong force, to call forth. It is a calling to one side. Peter didn't preach, sit down, cross his legs, and look humble. He didn't preach and say, "Now let's sing a hymn, and if by chance anyone might possibly want to step forward for Christ, you can do so at this time, but please don't feel like you have to." Peter did not apologize. What did he do? He gave a gospel invitation. When he finished with his sermon, he pleaded for souls. "With many other words he pleaded with them."

Dr. W. A. Criswell, the God-anointed pastor of First Baptist Church, Dallas, advises us well.

> As a famous London pastor lay dying, his friends gathered around and asked, "Do you have one last word for the world?" The loving pastor replied: "Yes, I do. Tell the pastors of the world this, 'Oh preacher, make it plain how a man can be saved!'"

> When the pastor has shown the sinner that he is lost, when he has presented Christ's redemptive plan of salvation, then he is to draw the penitent into an open confession of his faith in Jesus (Matt. 10:32-33; Rom. 10:9-10). How does he do that effectively? How can the pastor extend an invitation that pulls at the heartstrings of a lost man? Here are some suggestions to consider:

> 1. It must be in the heart of the preacher to make an appeal to people. He must pray to this end that God will help him do it effectively . . .

2. The sermon must lead up to this climactic consumma-
   tion. Whatever the subject, the message must be turned
   to the soul for the grace and mercy of God . . .

3. Many pastors close their sermons with a prayer while
   the heads of the people are bowed in prayer with him. In
   this prayer this pastor prays for the lost and for others
   who are to be included in the invitation . . .

4. At the end of the prayer the congregation can be asked
   to stand as the choir begins to sing the invitation
   hymn . . .

5. The invitation can be for anything the Spirit lays upon
   the heart of the pastor. Besides the appeal for the lost to
   confess their faith in the Lord, the invitation can be for
   baptism and church membership, the transfer of church
   letters, those who cannot get church letters to come forward by statement . . .

6. Music plays an all-important part in this appeal . . .[15]

There should always be an appeal *after* the gospel is
preached. The reverse is also true. The gospel should
always be preached *before* an appeal is given. We should
never issue an appeal until after the gospel is preached.

Many of us have heard evangelists who tell one death-
bed story after another, moving on the emotions of the hearers, never having within their message the "kerygma"
—the fact that He who knew no sin became sin for us that
we might become the righteousness of God in Him. There is
considerable fall-out of "new converts" due to this. Peter
preached the gospel and then made an appeal; such is biblical and right. He pleaded for souls that day. He exhorted
them. "With many words" he besought them with strong
force to receive Christ.

He pleaded with them to "save yourselves from this corrupt generation." Although God takes the initiative, God *chooses, calls, convicts,* and *converts,* and *we* must *confess.* We must identify with the Lord Jesus Christ. Paul said it this way, "For with the heart man believeth unto righteousness; and with the mouth confession is made unto salvation" (Rom. 10:10, KJV). Peter was calling for a decision. "With many other words he warned them; and he pleaded with them, 'Save yourselves from this corrupt generation'" (Acts 2:40).

For the true preacher of the gospel, preaching is not a profession; it is an obsession. In a sense, that is true for every believer. Every waking minute it is a part of our lives. Our proclamation must be *persistent.* There is a note of urgency here. What makes a church great in the eyes of God? The element of *participation* and also the element of *proclamation.* Our preaching must be *prophetic, plain, positive, penetrating, persuasive, pointed, pious,* and *persistent.*

Productive Proclamation

Tenth, it must also be productive. Acts 2:41 reported, "Those who accepted his message were baptized, and about three thousand were added to their number that day." Three thousand precious persons were saved that day and followed the Lord in believer's baptism. It is apparent that the Bible doesn't speak a word about these newly baptized believers speaking in *glossa.* Although Acts 2:38 shows, "you will receive the gift of the Holy Spirit."

No doubt most of those converts at Pentecost were Jews. So far as we know, the first church was largely made up of Jews. It is wrong to think that all the Jews in the first century rejected the Christian religion. No! They were the first ones who really accepted Him. They accepted all that the prophets had foretold about the Messiah, and many saw Him as Jesus of Nazareth.

The truth about the Christian church is we don't ask Jewish people to convert to our religion; we have converted to theirs. The Lord Jesus is indeed the Jewish Messiah. Had you visited the first church in Jerusalem (30 A.D.), you would have found it comprised almost totally of Jewish believers.

Some today insist that Jews have a special way of being saved apart from the Lord Jesus Christ. But Peter preached to them, "repent" (Acts 2:38). He called on them to change their minds about themselves, the Savior, their sin, and salvation. To whom was he speaking? Jews! Religious Jews. He was not afraid he would offend them. There are preachers today who will not even pray in the name of Jesus if Jewish people are present for fear of offending them. Listen to Peter as he answered their question of what they should do with the word "repent!"

Three thousand people were saved in one day! They did so much with so little, and we seem to do so little with so much! What a gorgeous picture here of Christ receiving sinners. He casts out none who trust in Him.

What makes a church great? The element of *participation* which involves unity and unction is vitally important. There has never been a great church in the eyes of God that didn't make Bible *proclamation* which was *prophetic, plain, positive, personal, penetrating, persuasive, pointed, pious, persistent,* and *productive.*

3
Preservation

Quite often, so many people in various places are touched with sparks of genuine revival, only to have them burn out because they are not preserved, and the flame is not "fanned." Preservation simply may be the lost word in our ecclesiastical vocabulary. Too many "converts" in too many churches go in the front door only to go out the back door, never to be seen again.

Frank was president of the bank across the street from our First Baptist Church downtown. Though we had never had a conversation, I had heard about his wife's ensuing struggle with cancer and its dismal prognosis. I called to make an appointment. Walking into his stately, mahogany-trimmed office, I sat down across from his desk and said, "I have heard about your wife and wondered if I might pray with you?"

This powerful businessman melted in the warmth of God's love. As his eyes began to fill with tears, he kept repeating, "Oh thank you, oh thank you, oh thank you." We prayed together, and in a few weeks Frank had found new life in Jesus Christ. His sweet wife went to heaven, and after the funeral

Frank enrolled in our "New Beginnings" discipleship ministry. For sixteen weeks he diligently attended all the classes
and passed with flying colors. Preserved and strengthened
by his new life, he is active in Bible study classes and never
misses a worship service.

We are discovering something exciting in our "First Family." There are over four hundred promises in the Bible to
those who will minister to the poor. We make a concentrated
effort to "go after" the kind of people that most other
churches seem not to want. We do it through our many street
ministries and clothing ministries.

But we are discovering that the easiest people to reach for
Christ are not the shadows of men and women who might
have been living on the streets, but the people behind the
mahogany doors of the high-rise offices. They have everything prosperity and position have to offer and know by experience that its promises are void and do not satisfy the needs
of the human heart.

Like Frank, they are waiting for someone to have the Christian courage to ask, "Can I pray with you?" And for someone
to hold them by the hand along the way of growing in the
Christian faith. If we are not as committed to preservation as
we are presentation, it will do us little good to plead, "Revive
us again!"

[41]Those who accepted his message were baptized, and about
three thousand were added to their number that day.

[42]They devoted themselves to the apostles' teaching and
to the fellowship, to the breaking of bread and to prayer.
[43]Everyone was filled with awe, and many wonders and miraculous signs were done by the apostles. [44]All the believers
were together and had everything in common. [45]Selling

their possessions and goods, they gave to anyone as he had need. ⁴⁶Every day they continued to meet together in the temple courts. They broke bread in their homes and ate together with glad and sincere hearts (Acts 2:41-46).

Great churches are not only made up of *participation* and *proclamation* but also *preservation*. The Bible says these early believers "devoted themselves" (Acts 2:42) and that they "continued steadfastly" (Acts 2:42, KJV). There are three elements involved in the *preservation* of new converts in the church of Jesus Christ. They are *baptism,* the *Bible,* and *body life*.

One can never grow to Christian maturity apart from the Bible. Perhaps the worst problem in many churches is a host of spiritual infants who have never grown in their faith.

Recently two eight-year-old boys were brought to Orlando to the world-famous Disney World. They each had a disease which aged their bodies far in advance of their years. While the boys were only children, their appearance was that of eighty-year-old men. They were children who had grown old and were about to die but had never grown up.

As I watched those two boys on the newscast, I thought about how so many are like that in the church today. They are children who have grown old in the faith but have never grown up. This is the tragedy of the twentieth-century church.

If you have ever had a baby in your home, there are some things you have readily observed. As much as you love them, babies do want their own way. They want what they want, when they want it! Also, you will note that babies seem basically lazy. That is, they lie around a lot.

They don't (and can't) wash any of the dishes, make any of the beds, or pick up any of the dirty clothes. The fact is they've simply not grown enough to make "mature" decisions and perform certain duties. Another obvious characteristic of a baby is that he or she is taken up with personalities. As far as we know, a baby can't look beyond a personality to have a spirit of discernment. The biggest mass murderer in America could come into their room and utter a few ga-ga's and goo-goo's and have a baby smiling. One of the most evident characteristics of a baby is that he can play while big things are happening. Some families can be going through the heartache of divorce or death, while all the time the baby is down on the floor playing with a ball. Finally, babies get easily upset. If you don't believe it, just don't give a baby a bottle at the time he thinks he needs it and see his reaction!

All of the above are signs of babes in Christ. They may be seventy years old, but if they have never matured in their faith, their feelings are the same spiritually as those babies are physically. Babies in the church always want their own way. They have no spirit of submission. They are not interested in what other church members think. Babies in the church are basically lazy. You will not find them out on outreach night or involved in other ministries.

Like physical babies, they do not give of themselves in the realm of time, talent, or tithe. Also, they are unconcerned about others. They are taken up with personalities. They have no spirit of discernment between the spirit of good and the spirit of wrong. One of the most tragic facts about babies in the church is that, like physical babies, they play when big things are happening. Tremendous transformations take place in people's lives, and people are saved and pass from darkness into light, but it really makes no difference to a spiritual baby since his greatest concern is getting to the cafeteria line and making sure the service does not go past noon. Spiritual babies also become upset easily.

We know what children need. All they need is to grow up! And it is impossible to grow up as a Christian apart from the Word of God. The early church preserved their new converts and the way they did it was through baptism, the Bible, and body life.

Believer's Baptism

The first important element in preservation is believer's baptism. In Acts 2:38-41, Peter called upon his hearers to "repent and be baptized." Why? Because it is essential in preservation. As soon as these early believers were saved, they were immediately baptized. This is throughout the Book of Acts.

Today, we often hear some people talk about the fact that a new convert has to "prove" himself before being baptized, but this was certainly not the case in the early church.

Acts 8 recorded the baptism of the Ethiopian eunuch:

Then Philip began with that very passage of Scripture and told him the good news about Jesus.

As they traveled along the road, they came to some water and the eunuch said, "Look, here is water. Why shouldn't I be baptized?" And he ordered the chariot to stop. Then both Philip and the eunuch went down into the water and Philip baptized him (vv. 35-38).

In Acts 10, there was baptism in the family of Cornelius: "'Can anyone keep these people from being baptized with

water? They have received the Holy Spirit just as we have'"
(v. 47).

In Acts 16, Lydia was baptized after her conversion:

> One of those listening was a woman named Lydia, a dealer
> in purple cloth from the city of Thyatira, who was a wor-
> shiper of God. The Lord opened her heart to respond to
> Paul's message. When she and the members of her house-
> hold were baptized, she invited us to her home. "If you con-
> sider me a believer in the Lord," she said, "come and stay at
> my house." And she persuaded us (vv. 14-15).

In the same chapter the Philippian jailer was gloriously
saved and immediately baptized:

> He then brought them out and asked, "Men, what must I do
> to be saved?"
> They replied, "Believe in the Lord Jesus, and you will be
> saved—you and your household." Then they spoke the word
> of the Lord to him and to all the others in his house. At that
> hour of the night the jailer took them and washed their
> wounds; then immediately he and his family were baptized
> (Acts 16:30-33).

What is baptism? It is a picture of death to the old life
and resurrection to walk in newness of life (see Rom. 6:4).
The truth of Scripture is you should be baptized as a confession of your faith as soon as possible after conversion. First
there is *conviction* (Acts 2:37). Then there is *conversion* and
confession (Acts 2:38). Baptism is confession for the believer. The reason many churches do not have preservation
in their membership, even though they may have participation and proclamation, is because of a lack of emphasis on
the first step of obedience, which is baptism.

Why does my denomination emphasize baptism so much? It is not because the water will wash away a single sin, but it is vitally important to spiritual growth and preservation. If we are not obedient to the first step of Christian growth, how are we ever going to grow? If we do not live up to the light God gives us, how are we going to expect any more light? It is no wonder that more Christians do not grow in the grace and knowledge of our Lord. So many say, "Well, I'm going to think about baptism for a while." Baptism is an essential step in preservation and Christian growth.

What is true New Testament baptism? It is best illustrated with the wedding ring. While wearing a wedding ring does not make one married, it certainly is an indication that one has made that commitment. On July 24, 1970, my wife gave me a wedding ring as we stood publicly at a wedding altar and committed our lives to each other. I have worn that ring every day since then as a means of identification regarding that commitment. She could have given me my wedding ring three months before we were married, and I could have worn it, but it would have meant nothing. Many people have been baptized before they made their commitment to Christ, were born again, and have really followed the Lord in believer's baptism, which must be subsequent to our time of commitment.

Baptism is commanded in the Great Commission (Matt. 28:19-20). It is the first public act of the believer in his confession of faith in Christ. It is ordinarily the door into the visible, local church. It is the initial ordinance (Acts 2:41; Acts 8:12; 1 Cor. 12:12-14; 1 Pet. 3:21). The act of baptism involves a personal obligation on the part of the believer to promote the cause of Christ represented by the work of the church. The true New Testament church is a soul-saving, baptizing, teaching, preaching, evangelistic institution, and the baptized believer is now a part of that great, missionary, worldwide ministry. We are united by the Spirit in the worship of God in praise, in thanksgiving, in prayer, and in the diffusion of the saving message of Christ to every creature. We are joined together in the body of our Lord for instruction, for spiritual growth, and for mutual helpfulness. It is a great, glorious, mighty, significant day when we are baptized into the body of Christ, the bride and church of our Lord.[1]

What then is the mode of New Testament baptism? The Greek word found here in the text is *baptizo*. It means to plunge, dip, submerge, or put under. It is used in the text no fewer than seventy-four times in the New Testament. This particular word which means to put under is not only found in the New Testament, it is extensively used in Greek literature. In Greek literature the word *baptizo* meant, in some cases, to suffer shipwreck, to sink, or to perish in the water. The story is told of a Greek sea captain whose vessel was going down and he broadcast this "mayday" message, "Baptizo, Baptizo!" (I'm sinking, I'm sinking!) Since our Lord has commanded us to be baptized, it is certainly imperative that we should desire the proper New Testament mode. This mode of baptism is immersion.

The word in the original language, found in Acts 2:41, means to immerse. It is as plain as the nose on your face when you read the Scripture. We read that baptism required "much water." Take for example John 3:23, "Now John also was baptizing at Aenon near Salim, because there was plenty of water, and people were constantly coming to be baptized." Baptism is described as a "going down into the water." "And he ordered the chariot to stop. Then both Philip and the eunuch went down into the water and Philip baptized him" (Acts 8:38).

New Testament baptism is like a "burial" under the water.

> We were therefore buried with him through baptism into death in order that, just as Christ was raised from the dead through the glory of the Father, we too may live a new life (Rom. 6:4).

> Now if we died with Christ, we believe that we will also live with him (Rom. 6:8).

New Testament baptism is described as coming up out of the water. "As soon as Jesus was baptized, he went up out of the water. At that moment heaven was opened, and he saw the Spirit of God descending like a dove and lighting on him" (Matt. 3:16).

The crystal-clear truth of Scripture is that baptism is by immersion. And it should always follow salvation! If you have not been immersed since your salvation experience you have not undergone New Testament baptism. This is not the view of any particular church. It is the truth of Scripture. Baptism should take place after salvation and not before. Note the order in Acts 2:38, "Repent and be baptized." The same order is found in Acts 2:41: "Those who accepted his message were baptized."

There are churches which practice infant baptism. Some churches baptize babies and very young children who have not yet had a genuine salvation experience. Many of these churches use Acts 2:39 as a proof text which goes: "The promise is for you and your children and for all who are far off—for all whom the Lord our God will call." They claim infants should be baptized. But what does Acts 2:39 really teach? Read it carefully. Some take this verse and put a period after the word "children" so that it reads, "The promise is for you and your children." Thus, they insist infants ought to be sprinkled; their argument being that the blessings of the covenant are for them and their children. But you cannot chop off a verse halfway and make it fit your own personal philosophy of theology.[2]

What is Acts 2:39 actually conveying? Look at it carefully. "The promise is for you and your children *and* for all those who are far off—for all whom the Lord our God will call" (author's italics). It is not only for you and your children, it is for those who are "far off." So then I may argue, "The promise is for you and your children": therefore your children should be baptized. If we go on with the text, "and for all those who are far off," then all who are far off should also be baptized. Therefore, we would be saying, all who are far off should be baptized whether they are saved or not. So goes this reasoning, and it is completely unbiblical!

What does this text actually mean? It is pointing out that this covenant promise, ". . . whosoever shall call on the name of the Lord shall be saved" (Acts 2:21, KJV), is meant for you and your children . . . and for those who are far off—the African natives, the negritos of New Guinea, the ebony-faced women of Ghana, the Eskimos in their igloos in Alaska, and anybody anywhere "to whom the Lord our God will call" is addressed. Someone quickly replies, "but whole households were baptized in the Book of Acts." Yes, but there is no scriptural reason to believe that in any case they did not first repent as Peter had preached in Acts 2:38. And after they had done this, then they were baptized!

Imagine the effect on Jerusalem when three thousand people came out of the shadows to identify with the Lord Jesus Christ through believer's baptism. It is no wonder the whole city was stirred and moved. It is no wonder spiritual awakening came to Jerusalem. The first step in preserving new converts is to see them through the waters of baptism. Peter unapologetically and personally appealed to his hearers to be baptized. Every church should exhort their converts to be baptized, not because the water would save them or wash away their sins, but because it is the first step in preservation, growing in the grace and knowledge of our Lord. The truth is if we do not live up to the light God has given us, we can never expect to receive any more light.

Baptism is a means of identification. There is a prevalent trend in our culture. People today like to identify with certain things or persons. Some people wear keyrings with Mercedes Benz emblems, while others wear Gucci shoes with its emblem. Still others would not think of carrying anything but a Mont Blanc pen, while others wouldn't wear a tie that was not a Hermes. People like to identify with their schools so they wear a class ring or class sweater. There are some who would not wear a sweater that did not have the emblem of Ralph Lauren. There are still others who are quick to identify with Rolex watches.

Baptism gives us an opportunity to do what we like to do. That is, identify with something. Or, rather in this case, someone! Baptism is a means of identification. It lets the world know we have identified with Jesus Christ. What makes a church great in the eyes of God? *Participation, proclamation,* and *preservation.* The first step in preservation is *baptism.*

The Bible

The second step in preservation is the Bible. "They devoted themselves to the apostles' teaching" (Acts 2:42). That is, they continued in the Word of God. The word *didache* means doctrine, or translated in the *New International Version* as teaching.[3]

This consisted of the fundamentals of the faith. They devoted themselves to such great doctrinal truths as the virgin birth of Christ, His sinless life and vicarious death, His bodily resurrection, and His second coming. They grounded themselves and continued in the great doctrinal truths of the Word of God.

We are not called merely to make decisions; we are called to make disciples. When a person is genuinely saved, one "continues in the apostles' teaching." Our Lord Himself observed, "By their fruits you shall know them." There can be no preservation in the church where the Bible, and its doctrine and teaching, are not expounded and explained to the people. Many wonder why membership dwindles in some churches. It is because God blesses His Word, and when it is not used, there is no preservation. The church exploded in Jerusalem because they "devoted themselves" and continued steadfastly "in the apostles' teaching." They were rooted and grounded in the Word of God. Our only hope for preservation is the Word of God. You cannot grow in faith without that Word. You may be saved and be baptized, but if you do not devote yourself to the apostles' teaching, you will never grow in the grace and knowledge of Jesus Christ. Paul wrote to Timothy that the Word of God was "profitable." This is throughout the Scriptures. In Romans, the Bible is profitable for *doctrine*. In the Corinthian letters, the Bible is profitable for *reproof*. In Galatians, the Bible is profitable for *correction*. In Ephesians, it is profitable for *instruction in righteousness*.

The Bible is like God's road map. *First, there is doctrine.* We begin down the road with Christ, and we face the amazing doctrinal truth of the Deity of Christ. He is God. When we obey and come to Christ, we are walking on the road with Him. But what happens when we veer along the road? *We see secondly that the Bible is profitable for reproof.* It reproves us and helps us recognize a wrong turn. God said, "'Is not my word like . . . a hammer that breaks a rock in pieces?'" (Jer. 23:29). How does one straighten out one's path? *Here we find the Bible is profitable for correction.* The word shows us how to get back on track with God, but it doesn't leave us there. *Finally, it is profitable for instruction in righteousness* (2 Tim. 3:16-17). The Word shows us how to stay on the road so we will not wander off again. It is profitable and essential in our preservation and growth.

On the night shift a young bivocational preacher was using his New Testament to witness during the company's 11:00 p.m. break. One of the listeners commented, "Yeah, just look at that guy leaning on his crutch."

To that the preacher replied, "You're right. It's my lifelong crutch, and I can't do anything without leaning on it! It's life-giving, powerful, and sharper than a two-edged sword. Yes, it's my crutch. It's a crutch for poor, crippled sinners, and it'll boost them into heaven!"

What if I say—
"The Bible is God's Holy Word,

Complete, inspired, without a flaw"—
    But let its pages stay,
Unread from day to day,
And fail to learn there from God's law;
What if I go out there to seek
    The truth of which I glibly speak,
    For guidance on this earthly way,—
    Does it matter what I say?[4]

What makes a church great? Participation, proclamation, and preservation, which entails making much of baptism and much of the Bible.

Body Life

The third important element in preservation is body life. This body life concept is found in Acts 2:42-46:

> They devoted themselves to the apostles' teaching and to the fellowship, to the breaking of bread and to prayer. Everyone was filled with awe, and many wonders and miraculous signs were done by the apostles. All the believers were together and had everything in common. Selling their possessions and goods, they gave to anyone as he had need. Every day they continued to meet together in the temple courts. They broke bread in their homes and ate together with glad and sincere hearts.

These people spent their time learning, loving, and listening to each other. Great churches are characterized by this body life concept. Every member is a minister and everyone functions within the body together. There was fellowship in this early church. "They devoted themselves to the apostles' teaching and to the *fellowship*" (Acts 2:42, author's italics). The word is *koinonia*. It means they were "all together," and they loved each other. It was one for all and all for one. It was a shared life.

The origin of the word *koinos* (from which *koinonia* is derived) means common, not in the sense we often think of today. It meant that which people share or have together. Consider the phrase, and they had all things common in relation to the Jerusalem church. Even in our current generation we often use the phrase, "We or they have such and such in common." It implies a like trait or characteristic.

All of us are familiar with metal money which is called a coin or coins. Those terms are straight from the Greek language. What is a coin used for? It is used for exchange, and it passes from hand to hand. Those who have phobias about germs probably think about a quarter, half dollar, or even pennies as possibly being soiled, because they have passed from hand to hand. A coin is a common piece shared by perhaps hundreds, maybe even thousands of hands.

Thus, it is with the *koinonia* we have in Christ. *Koinonia* ideally means, not merely fellowship, but a life which is shared. Every born-again, blood-bought believer has a common Savior, faith, experience, goal, and destiny. Wherever you meet another genuine Christian, you have an immediate spiritual tie. If only we could remember this, churches would have virtually no real problems because all Christians are together through "the scarlet thread" of the blood of Jesus Christ which has drawn us and sewn us together into God's tapestry of the redeemed.

Koinonia is not merely coming together to have a meal or to participate in church activities. What a word . . . "what a fellowship, what a joy divine, leaning on the everlasting arms."

When a person is born again into God's family, he immediately has a kinship to every believer here and in the here-after!

What happened? The coming and filling of the Holy Spirit caused them to live life on a higher plane of love for God and for one another. There are different Greek words which are translated into our English Bible with the word *love*. There is the word *agape* which means giving, forgiving, unreserved, or self—God's love. There is also *philos* which means tender affection, the brotherly sort of love. Prior to Pentecost, the best the apostles could do was to love on the level of *philos*. In fact, that is the best anyone can do without the Holy Spirit in his or her heart.

For example, you remember the conversation of our Lord Jesus with Simon Peter on the shore before Pentecost. John 21:15 records it. The Lord asked him, "Simon, son of John, do you love me more than these?" The word He used was *agape*.

Simon answered. "Yes, Lord, you know that I love you." Peter replied with the word *phileo*. It was the best Peter could do.[5]

Then on the night before the crucifixion, Jesus instructed His apostles,

> "A new command I give you: Love one another. As I have loved you, so you must love one another. All men will know that you are my disciples if you love one another" (John 13:34-35).

Here is the word *agape*. Jesus was leaving His followers. They had watched His life for three years and up until then, the best they could do was to love on the level of *philos* love. It was the level of the old commandment which taught to "'love your neighbor as yourself'" (Lev. 19:18). But now, love was not an option. It was to be a new commandment. It was to be *agape* and not philos. The point is this: Prior to Pentecost one could not love properly with God's love, because it is impossible without the Spirit's love burning within us. This love came into the disciples when they were filled with the Holy Spirit, and thus they "continued steadfastly, devoting themselves to fellowship." This is why Paul later wrote in Galatians 5:22, "the fruit of the Spirit is love" *(agape)*.

There was a legend that a rich merchant scoured the Mediterranean world looking for the distinguished apostle Paul. He encountered Timothy, the legend goes, who arranged a visit with Paul, who was a prisoner in Rome at that time.

Entering the jail cell, the merchant found a rather old man, physically broken down. The merchant was amazed at Paul's personal peace and serenity. The story goes that they talked for hours. The merchant left with Paul's blessing and prayer on his heart and mind. Outside the concerned merchant inquired, "What is the key to Paul's power? I have never seen anyone like him in my entire life."

"Haven't you figured it out?" asked Timothy. "Paul is in love."

The businessman with bewilderment asked, "In love?"

"Yes," Timothy answered, "Paul is in love with Jesus Christ."

The man looked even more confused. "Is that all?" he further inquired.

With a smile on his face, the young preacher answered, "Ah, but that is everything."

This has so many applications. For example, this is why it is essential for a Christian to marry another believer and not an unbeliever. Try as he may, an unbeliever can never love a mate with the highest level of love, the most selfless kind of love *(agape)*, because it is only found in Jesus Christ.

We need each other. Great churches are made up of great fellowship. We can be baptized and be in the Bible but still cannot grow without this concept of body life—*fellowship*. We need each other. There has never been a great church in the eyes of God without this element of fellowship. Some "professed believers" have such little fellowship with the people of God. We all ought to ask ourselves if we are merely singing hymns, saying words, and coming to meetings, just going through the motions. Some of us live like the world, think like the world, talk like the world, act like the world, and then go to church, watch our watches, and if the service goes over an hour we fidget. At the same time, we can go to a ball game, movie, or party and say, "How time flies," when we have been there three hours or more. And you tell me you are going to go to heaven, praise the Lord, and fellowship with the people of God there when you don't desire that fellowship here. Who are you kidding? Yourself!

What makes a great church? Participation, proclamation, and preservation. Preservation involves baptism, the Bible, and body life. The first part of body life is *fellowship,* but there is also the importance of the *"breaking of bread"* (Acts 2:42, author's italics). That is the Lord's Supper. Luke does not simply refer to having meals together. He makes the point that the early church came together to share in the symbolic testimony of the body and blood of Christ which is the basis of the Christian life. What is the breaking of bread? It is the Lord's Supper—the unleavened bread and the cup of unfermented juice from the vine. We have continued in this until this very day. It is a part of our preservation.

> Thy supper, Lord, before us spread,
> The cup beside the broken bread,
> Reminds us of Thy life laid down—
> The shameful cross, the thorny crown.
>
> Thy sacrifice was for our gain;
> To save us Thou didst bear the pain.
> Thy love is clear for all to see;
> We bow in thankful prayer to Thee.
>
> In fellowship with Thee we feel
> That Thou art here, Thy presence real;
> Thou hast risen and dost live
> Within our hearts, new life to give
>
> Now may the worship we know here
> Remind us always thou art near;
> Help us to live our lives each day
> In love and faith,
> O Lord, we pray.
>
> Author Unknown

They also devoted themselves to "prayer" (see Acts 2:42). They continued in prayer. This is how they began. For ten days they prayed in the upper room. Some of us begin but never continue. Please note that they "devoted themselves" to prayer, not just in teaching, fellowship, and breaking of bread, but to prayer, beseeching the Lord at the throne of grace.

They also had a sharing spirit. Acts 2:42-44 says,

They devoted themselves to the apostles' teaching and to
the fellowship, to the breaking of bread and to prayer.
Everyone was filled with awe, and many wonders and miraculous signs were done by the apostles. All the believers
were together and had everything in common.

They had the theme that every member was a minister. I
doubt if they said, "Let Peter do it," or "Let's let Joseph of
Arimathea pull a string with the United Way of Jerusalem." Everyone was together, and they all did their part.

Some contend that this sounds like communism. This
was not communism in Acts 2. These people believed in
God; this was church-controlled and not state-controlled;
it was voluntary; and it was obviously temporary. Many
Jews were away from home in Jerusalem for the Passover
Feast. We do not read about it happening later in the early
church, but the point is they had this concept of body life!
What is the difference in what we see here and in communism today? Communism says, "What's yours is mine."
This sharing in the Jerusalem church stated, "What's mine
is yours."[6] And this is a stark difference! And that is why
communism is crumbling all over the world.

Everything the believers owned was at God's disposal
when needed. This is the point. Is everything we own at
God's disposal today? What if God were to impress upon
your heart to give a certain amount of your stock portfolio or
your real estate holdings? What if God were to impress
upon you to give that precious possession to share it with
the fellowship of believers?

These early believers "continued steadfastly in prayers."
Prayer is the cradle of revival. Jesus said, "My house shall
be called the house of prayer." So many believers get

dressed up in the whole armor of God of Ephesians 6. We put on the helmet of salvation and the breastplate of righteousness while holding the shield of faith and the sword of the Spirit which is the Word of God. We also have around our loins the girdle of truth and on our feet shoes with the preparation of the gospel of peace. We are ready to go for God.

But the problem often lies in the fact that many of us don't even know where the battle is being fought. After telling us all the pieces of the armor, Paul links armor with prayer in the next verse "Praying always with all prayer and supplication in the Spirit" (Eph. 6:18, KJV).

Prayer is the battlefield of the Christian life. It is impossible to win a war unless we march to the field. Consequently, the most important ministry of a local church should be the ministry of prayer. The most important room in all of the physical facilities of our First Baptist Church in Fort Lauderdale is our Intercessory Prayer Chapel, where so many of our people "stand in the gap" and intercede to the Father on behalf of our members and ministries. We make much of prayer in our fellowship.

In fact, before every great undertaking, we have days of prayer and fasting. The first committee appointed during our recent multimillion-dollar building program was a prayer committee which continually kept prayer needs before our people week by week. Our Sunday morning services begin with our men on their knees at the altar beseeching the God of heaven for His power to fall upon us. Our Wednesday evening services conclude with hundreds of people at the altar praying for the lost and for physical, emotional, and spiritual needs as we "pray for one another." Yes, Jesus said that His house was to be called "the house of prayer." The heart-cry, "Revive us again," will never be realized unless it is ushered in on the wings of personal intercessory prayer.

Another concept of body life was "gladness and singleness of heart" (Acts 2:46, KJV). This was a joyful church. A gloomy Christian is a contradiction in terms. Joy filled the atmosphere of the presence of these people at Pentecost.

Another aspect of their body life was worship and praise (Acts 2:46-47). Praise is the secret of the liberated life! There is power in praise. "God inhabits the praises of his people," and we are to praise Him in song, word, and action. The truth is we cannot grow in grace and knowledge of our Lord without being involved in personal praise. In Ephesians 5:18, we find the command, "be filled with the Spirit," and in the next verse we notice the result in "singing and making melody in our hearts to the Lord" (Eph. 5:19, KJV).

What makes a church great in the eyes of God? *Participation* and *proclamation* but also *preservation*. How is this preservation obtained? Through *baptism,* the *Bible,* and *body-life* concept.

4
Propagation

In the eyes of most people, Jim was too old to be useful. And besides, for the most part, he had blown his reputation. His family had settled Fort Lauderdale back in the last generation, when there was nothing here but beaches, swamps, and Indians. He had been through a fortune and had virtually nothing to show for it. He had fought alcoholism for years and usually lost. At almost seventy years of age, life had little purpose left for this pitiful pioneer.

But like thousands of others in our church during the past decade, Jim met Jesus and did things ever change! He soon enrolled in our evangelism training ministry and learned to share his faith. A soul-winner's fire and passion began to consume him, and the propagation of the gospel became his daily desire. Today, Jim personally leads to faith in Christ over one hundred adults a year, and he has trained scores of additional "soul-winners" who are winning many others. He is presenting and developing a new ministry which will enable us to propagate more effectively the gospel and preserve new converts and all of this after his seventieth birthday!

Our First Baptist Church has almost one hundred ongoing ministries which have originated with and are carried on by our lay members who have discovered their spiritual gifts and have come to realize that God has a job for them that no one else can do quite like they can. While we may have scores of varied ministries, we still have only one purpose—to fulfill the Great Commission by making, marking, and maturing new believers. And this begins with the propagation of the gospel of the Lord Jesus Christ. Jim is walking, talking, and living proof that God can use any of us when we fully yield to him and earnestly beseech the throne of heaven as we pray, "Revive us again!"

> Praising God and enjoying the favor of all the people. And the Lord added to their number daily those who were being saved (Acts 2:47).

A church can have participation, proclamation, and preservation, but if the church does not have the element of propagation, it will never be a great church in the eyes of God. This early church went everywhere witnessing. The propagation of the gospel fulfilled Acts 1:8 in one day. And the result was the "Lord added to their number daily those who were being saved." They propagated the gospel in a winsome way and a winning way.

If we are ever to see the church truly revived again in our generation, then we must lay hold of this concept of equipping the saints to do the work of the ministry. This first-century church went everywhere sharing their faith and performing the works of ministry.

The churches in our day and age who are seeing mercy drops of revival are those who have mobilized their people to do the work of ministry. These are churches which have all kinds of ministries but only one overriding purpose, and that is to glorify and honor the Lord Jesus by fulfilling the Great Commission to make, mark, and mature believers in the faith.

Example

To begin with, mobilization is done by example. If pastors are going to mobilize their people as we move the church toward the twenty-first century, then we must be on the cutting edge ourselves, and our people must see that we do not ask them to do something we are too good to do ourselves. The best way to mobilize people for the work of ministry is by *example*. Perhaps Gideon expressed it best when, as he led his small army to face the Midianites, he said, "Do as I do!" These pointed words may be the epitaph of many churches today. That is, they do what the pastor does. My pastor used to tell all of his preacher boys: "Never use your people to build your ministry, but always use your ministry to build your people."

Expectancy

Another important element in the mobilization of people to the work of the ministry is expectancy. Here is the spirit of conquest. A vision, if you please. Someone has commented that a "vision without a task is simply a dream. A task without a vision is drudgery. But a vision with a task is the hope of the world."

Environment

Another key element in the mobilization of people to propagate the gospel is found in the word *environment*. In my opinion the two greatest factors in church growth are love and unity among the fellowship. This hurting, wounded world is looking for true love and true unity.

On the evening before the crucifixion, Jesus said, "A new commandment I give unto you, That ye love one another; *as I have loved you*" (John 13:34, KJV, author's italics). For thirty-three years Jesus had given us a picture of what real love truly is. Up until then, the best we could do was live on the level of the old commandment found in Leviticus 19:18, "Love your neighbor as yourself." But some of us have a real problem there. That is, we have no self-worth or self-respect, and if we loved others as we love ourselves, we wouldn't be loving with very deep love. But after thirty-three years of demonstrating what true love really is, Jesus said, "Love one another as I have loved you." The environment of love is the most important ingredient in church growth, and it is also the most basic factor in mobilizing people to propagate the gospel.

Not only is love important to the environment but also to unity. I believe the pastor's primary job is to "maintain the unity of the spirit and the bond of peace." Personally, this business is what I guard more than all else in our church—unity. The most important factor in a family is unity. The most important factor in an athletic team is unity. The most important factor in a business is unity. And a church should be known by its unity. I am not speaking about uniformity but unity. There is a tremendous difference. Uniformity is an outward expression while unity is an inward expression. Cults emphasize uniformity, not unity. There is diversity in unity. We are not all alike, but we can all be together.

Exertion

Another important word in mobilizing people to the propagation of the gospel is exertion. We are to equip the saints to do "the work of the ministry." And the ministry is work! When we are truly walking in the Spirit, we will not be wearing out the seats of our pants but the soles of our shoes. So often I hear that this church or that church simply operates "in the flesh." Well, the fact is, that is what our Spirit-filled lives have to operate within.

Do you know how hot and humid it can be in Fort Lauderdale in August? Our staff goes on soul-winning visits every Saturday. Often when I pull up in front of someone's house to share Jesus Christ only to have a door slammed in my face or to have someone rudely cut me off, my flesh does not advise me to keep doing that. My flesh tells me to go back home and sit under the air conditioner or lie down on a mat in the swimming pool. My flesh never told me to do anything for Christ. People will respond to exertion. They want to be a part of something exciting.

As we follow the life of Jesus, we discover that He exerted Himself so many times in so many ways. He had a special affinity toward the outcast. Jesus loves the rejects and pariahs of society. When He went to Jerusalem, where did He go? To the pool of Bethesda where handicapped persons were lying near the pool. When He went through Jericho where did He go? Did He make a beeline to meet the mayor to receive the key to the city? No, He went to a blind beggar rattling a cup on the side of the road. When He passed through Samaria did He have an "I-know-the-governor syndrome" like so many of us preachers today? No, He didn't go to the governor. He was interested in a sinful woman outside the city at Jacob's Well. He met her in the middle of the day to give her living water. Some of us need to stop being so hypocritical as we sit pompously behind our stained-glass walls talking about how much we care

about missions in blackest Africa when we are uncomfortable having a Haitian refugee sitting beside us on the pew.
Revival comes when folks do not mind getting their hands
dirty in something that is real.

Encouragement

We also find that another element of mobilizing people to
the propagation of the gospel is encouragement. Nothing
mobilizes people more than encouragement, words of ap-
preciation, exhortation, and encouragement. As we read
the Book of Acts, we find those early believers continually
encouraging one another in the faith. If the church is going
to be revived again in our day, it is not enough simply to
have the element of participation or proclamation or preservation. We must become caught up in propagation and
burst outside the four walls of our buildings, mobilizing our
people to do the work of the ministry and carrying the gospel to the four corners of the world!

Note that they propagated the gospel in a winsome way.
The Bible says they were "enjoying the favor of all the people" (Acts 2:47). The religious system of the day rejected
these early believers. They were a threat to the traditional
religion. Also, the Roman government rejected them because they would not bow down and say, "Caesar is Lord."
But the truth is that most of the people embraced them.
They "enjoyed the favor of all the people." They were winsome in their witness and in their worship, and thousands
were converted because of it.

Real Christianity is lovely. There is a quality about a
Spirit-filled, radiant Christian that draws and attracts
others and causes them to "enjoy favor with all the people."
The truth is that the gospel is not nearly as offensive as

some of its proponents! People were attracted to these early believers' joy and wanted to know the source of it. Evangelism in this first-century church was more caught than taught. And, that is how it should be in the twentieth-century church.

They also propagated the gospel in a winning way. "And the Lord added to their number daily those who were being saved" (Acts 2:47). They were a growing church! Every once in awhile we hear someone remark, "I like to be part of a small, spiritual church." There is no such thing as a small, spiritual church in a metropolitan area. I understand that population makes a difference. If the church is spiritual, it will be healthy, and if it is healthy, it will be growing! If you are the type of person who does not want to be part of a large church, you certainly would not have wanted to be a member of the first church in Jerusalem in the first-century.

What do I mean? Let's see! In Acts 1:15, there were 120 believers. Someone says, "Oh, we like it like that." There are many churches like that. They are often governed by people who want something they can control. Often they cannot control anything at work or at home, so they might join a little church and develop a "God complex." They want to be served; they don't want to serve. They want a preacher to stroke them and pat them on the back. All the while the whole world is going to hell, and they want a church they can control. This early church was a healthy church, and because it was healthy it was filled with participation, proclamation, preservation, and it propagated the gospel so it grew in grace and numbers.

Here we see these early believers being faithful to our Lord's last words to them, "But you will receive power

when the Holy Spirit comes on you; and you will be my witnesses in Jerusalem, and in all Judea and Samaria, and to
the ends of the earth" (Acts 1:8).

They had come to grips with five important questions
which had arisen out of these last words of our Lord. Now,
having been endued with power from on high, they were
fulfilling Acts 1:8 in their generation.

First, they dealt with the question of *who*. Here is an imperative in the future tense. No one was excluded. The
point is, none of us are beyond this commission of Christ to
be witnesses of His saving grace.

Next we deal with the question of *what*. They were to receive what? Power! Here is the urgent need of the church
today. Many churches are anemic in their worship and in
their witness. The word translated *power (dunamis)* is the
same word from which we receive our word *dynamite*. It
may be that the difference in the first-century church and
the twentieth-century church is in two words—influence
and power. While the church of our day prides itself in influence (particularly in the political realm), it has so little
power. The early church did not have enough influence to
keep Peter out of prison but had enough power to pray him
out!

Next, they dealt with the question of *when*. When? When
would this power come upon them? "When the Holy Spirit
comes upon you." The Holy Spirit within is Who gives
power. We need to strengthen our witness that comes from
a source that is outside of us. We need the dynamic power of
the Holy Spirit within us, and when we are being filled
with the Holy Spirit, witnessing will become as natural as
water running downhill. Like Peter and the other apostles,

we cannot "help but speak the things we have seen and heard."

They also dealt with the question of *why*. Why were they to receive power when the Holy Spirit came upon them? There is only one reason—"To be my witnesses." If you are saved, you have Christ, and He has you. If you have Christ, you have the Holy Spirit. If you have the Holy Spirit, you have power. If you have power, you are a witness. Note that He does not fill us with the Holy Spirit in order for us to become the judge, prosecuting attorney, defense, or jury—but the witness.

We are witnesses unto Christ. We are not recruiters trying to induce people to join our club. We are not salesmen trying to sell people our products. We are witnesses of Jesus Christ and His saving grace. The mark of a carnal church is that it talks about itself and invites people to come hear its preacher or to attend its Sunday School. The mark of a mature church is that it talks about the Lord Jesus Christ and is a witness unto Him.

This early church also dealt with the question of *where*. Where is this gospel to be taken as we are filled with God's Holy Spirit? The gospel is to be taken across the city, across the country, across the continent, and across the cosmos. There is a sense in which Acts 1:8 is an outline for the rest of the Book. They took the gospel to Jerusalem in Acts 1—8. They took the gospel through Judea and Samaria in Acts 9—12. They took the gospel to the ends of the earth in Acts 13—28. In thirty years this exciting early church fulfilled Acts 1:8. There is an important point for the church of our day. We cannot play leapfrog with the Great Commission. Witnessing for Christ begins in our own Jerusalem, not the ends of the earth. The highest form of hypocrisy is for mission groups to talk about how much they want to win people to Christ on foreign fields when they will not even share Jesus Christ with their next-door neighbor. Propagating the gospel begins at home and continues until it reaches the end of the world!

Many lament that taking the gospel to the whole world is a mammoth task for the twentieth-century church. What a task it must have been for the first-century church.

It looked *geographically* impossible. Many believed the world was still flat! It appeared to be *physically* impossible. There was no air travel, no printing press, no radio, no television, no telephone, and no fascimile machine. It looked *legally* impossible. It was against the law to speak in Christ's name in many places. It looked *socially* impossible. The church was made up of so many rejects and outcasts of society.

But how did they do it? They received power when the Holy Spirit came upon them and then they propagated the gospel to the ends of the world. They went where people are in need of the gospel of Jesus Christ.

The church must do this if it is ever going to be revived again. We need to remember Jesus did not die in a starched white shirt and tie on a gold cross on some white communion table within the stained-glass walls of some high-steeple church. He died where thieves were cursing and soldiers were gambling, and that is where we are to go, "to the ends of the earth." We are to penetrate the whole world until "the darkness shall turn to dawning. And the dawning to noon day bright. And Christ's great kingdom shall come on earth, the kingdom of love and light."

By Acts 2:41, we read "three thousand were added to

their number that day." Now there were 3,000 and 120. In Acts 2:47, it says, "the Lord added to their number daily." In Acts 4:4, "the number of men grew to about five thousand." The word for men used in Acts 4:4 is *andros*. It is a word used for man in the masculine sense as opposed to a woman. These were five thousand *men,* and it is likely their families were also saved. Some believe as many as fifteen to twenty thousand were saved by the time of this account in Acts 4:4. It is very possible then that the church numbered around 25,000 members. In Acts 5:28, we read that the message of Christ had "filled Jerusalem." Oh, what a day!

If only in our cities of America today, we might one day hear that our cities were filled with the good news of Jesus. In Acts 6:7, the number of disciples "increased rapidly." King James translators rendered this verse to read "multiplied greatly." Now, we are no longer talking about addition but multiplication. How many were in the early church? While no one knows for sure, Dr. B. H. Carroll, the founder of Southwestern Baptist Theological Seminary, thought there were 65,000 members the first six months. G. Campbell Morgan, the late, great pastor of Westminster Chapel in London, figures there were 250,000 converted in the first six months of the church in Jerusalem. The point is they propagated the gospel in a winsome way and in a winning way.

What makes a church great in the eyes of God? Participation, proclamation, preservation, and propagation. And we must have all four! There are some churches who have participation. They live together in unity and make much of the filling of the Holy Spirit but have no preservation. There are others who have proclamation and make much of the Bible but who have no participation, no sense of belonging to God, much less to one another. There are still others who make much of propagation but who have no sense of preservation of new converts. Great churches in the eyes of God, like the Jerusalem church, are characterized by a balanced ministry that involves all four elements. This is what the church needs today. Oh, that the church of Jesus Christ today would live together in unity, be filled with the Holy Spirit, make much of the Word of God in proclamation, preserve their new converts to grow in grace and knowledge, and go outside the four walls of their church to propagate the gospel in a winsome and winning way. If this would only happen, our land would be filled with the message of Jesus Christ.

One of the blessings of my own personal devotional life is to pray the great hymns of the faith. As I concluded these writings of the early church I found myself praying through my spirit the words of that great old hymn:

> Lord, as of old at Pentecost
> Thou didst Thy power display
> With cleansing purifying flame
> Descend on us today.

> For mighty words for Thee
> Prepare and strengthen every heart
> Come, take possessions of Thine own
> And never more depart.

> All self consume, all sin destroy
> With earnest zeal endue
> Each waiting heart to work for Thee
> O Lord, our faith renew.

Speak, Lord! Before Thy throne we wait
Thy promise we believe
And will not let thee go until
Thy blessing we receive.

Lord, send the old time power
The Pentecostal power
Thy flood gates of blessing
On us throw open wide.

Lord, send the old time power
The Pentecostal power
That sinners be converted
And Thy name glorified.

Lyrics by CHARLES H. GABRIEL

May God's special blessings rest upon that church which manifests its ministry in participation, proclamation, preservation, and propagation. And may our continual prayer be with that of the Psalmist: "O, that You would . . . REVIVE US AGAIN!"

Notes

Introduction

1. C. E. Matthews, *A Church Revival* (Nashville: Broadman Press, 1955), 20-21.

Chapter 1

1. *Life Application Bible* (Wheaton, Ill.: Tyndale Publishers, Inc., 1986), 305.

2. Fritz Reinecker and Cleon Rogers, *Linguistic Key to the Greek New Testament* (Grand Rapids, Mich.: Zondervan Publishing House, 1976), 265.

3. W. A. Criswell, *Acts an Exposition* (Grand Rapids, Mich.: Zondervan Publishing House, 1978), 77-78.

4. Ibid., 79.

Chapter 2

1. Lloyd John Ogilvie, *Acts: The Communicator's Commentary* (Waco, Tx.: Word Books, 1983), 70.

2. Words, Gloria and William J. Gaither. © Copyright 1971 by William J. Gaither. All rights reserved. Used by permission.

3. C. H. Spurgeon, *The Treasure of the New Testament II* (Grand Rapids, Mich.: Zondervan Publishing House, 1950), 745.

4. O. S. Hawkins, *Where Angels Fear to Tread* (Nashville: Broadman Press, 1983), 84-85.

5. Reinecker and Rogers, 267.

6. L. R. Scarborough, *With Christ After the Lost* (Nashville: Broadman Press, 1955), 55-56.

7. Ibid., 64.

8. Ibid., 65-66.

9. Ibid., 69, 71.

10. Ogilvie, 72.

11. H. L. Wilmington, *Wilmington's Guide to the Bible* (Wheaton, Ill.: Tyndale House Publishers, Inc., 1981), 371.

12. Criswell, 96.

13. John F. Walvoord and Roy B. Zuck, *The Bible Knowledge Commentary* (Wheaton, Ill.: Victor Books, 1983), 359.

14. Fanny J. Crosby, "Rescue the Perishing," *Baptist Hymnal* (Nashville: Convention Press, 1975), 285.

15. W. A. Criswell, *Criswell's Guidebook for Pastors* (Nashville: Broadman Press, 1980), 237-38.

Chapter 3

1. Criswell, *Guidebook,* 203.

2. Spurgeon, 747.

3. Criswell, *Acts,* 108.

4. Maud Frazer Jackson, *Masterpieces from Religious Verse,* ed. James Dalton Morrison (Nashville: Broadman Press, 1971), 383.

5. Ogilvie, 61.

6. Wilmington, 371.